BATTLE READY:
DEVOTIONAL DISCIPLESHIP

BATTLE READY: DEVOTIONAL DISCIPLESHIP

Spiritual Training for the Soldier of the Cross Volume 2

CHAPLAIN LANCE DIXON

ISBN:	Hardcover	978-1-5434-8073-3
	Softcover	978-1-5434-8072-6
	eBook	978-1-5434-8071-9

KJV
Scripture quotations marked KJV are from the Holy Bible, King James Version (Authorized Version). First published in 1611. Quoted from the KJV Classic Reference Bible, Copyright © 1983 by The Zondervan Corporation.

Any people depicted in stock imagery provided by Thinkstock are models, and such images are being used for illustrative purposes only. Certain stock imagery © Thinkstock.

Print information available on the last page.

Rev. date: 01/25/2018

To order additional copies of this book, contact:
Xlibris
1-888-795-4274
www.Xlibris.com
Orders@Xlibris.com
773590

CONTENTS

Dedication

This devotional book is dedicated to my wife Ashley, my daughter Taylor, and my son Garrett. Since the release of *Battle Ready* volume one, I have experienced a considerable amount of adversity, persecution, and spiritual testing and have found the testing fulfilling and strengthening. Most importantly, I have grown in my knowledge of the Gospel and God's grace. Before the church, God created the family, and it's the responsibility of every mother and father to train their children in godliness and discipline them according to the correct doctrines of the Bible by righteous conduct empowered by the Holy Spirit. Since the birth of my children, I have poured the Holy Scriptures into their minds and sought to model a lifestyle that honors Christ and exemplifies His compassion and mercy. Nevertheless, because of my own fallen nature, I have often failed to lead them as the Spirit has instructed me; however, I continue to strive after my duty to prepare them to enter a dark and depraved world. I have used my own struggles to teach them of the depths of human sin and their desperate need for God's grace. Thus, it's because of my children and their earthly and eternal future that I write these devotions. My love for Jesus and my responsibility to lead them inspire me to exegete the scriptures for their spiritual growth and preparation. It is my duty to prepare them to live in a world that is unfair, unforgiving, and exceptionally degenerate—a world that is ruled by Satan and his spiritual forces who want to control their thoughts and destroy their lives.

With a boundless desire for my family's understanding of the Gospel and their eternal destiny, I dedicate volume two of *Battle Ready* to Ashley, Taylor, and Garrett.

And he said unto me, My grace is sufficient for thee:
for my strength is made perfect in weakness.
Most gladly therefore will I rather glory in my infirmities,
that the power of Christ may rest upon me.
2 Corinthians 12:9

Introduction

A soldier of the cross never stops training, serving, praying, and seeking after Christ. Thus, I am honored to present volume two of *Battle Ready*. *Battle Ready* is part devotion, part Bible study. It's designed to demonstrate the divine authority of the individual verses of scripture by exegetically clarifying the deep meaning of each verse in a devotional format. Aptly named *Battle Ready*, the title declares the critical need for soldiers of the cross to prepare themselves, through the divine knowledge of God's Word, for the spiritual battles they will encounter in life. As each verse is magnified, believers are strengthened with divine understanding that equips them in their pursuit of truth and righteousness, based upon the orthodox theology of the early church fathers. *Battle Ready* is a Gospel-centered devotion that discipline, challenges, and encourages believers to examine the depth of God through His Holy Scriptures. Christ is elevated, and original human sin is understood from its origin in heaven and its arrival on earth. The traps and schemes of Satan are identified so followers of Christ are informed of the enemy's tactics and ready for spiritual battle. *Battle Ready* will provide readers with a hunger for God's Word and facilitate intense and direct interaction with the Gospel. Ultimately, *Battle Ready* is for mature believers and those who are looking to be challenged by the depths of the Holy Scriptures. It's written for the humble and those who desire spiritual growth beyond the superficial, feel-good devotional books that currently exist.

God's greatness is unsearchable; He is gracious, compassionate, and He guards all those who love Him (Psalm 145). Therefore, a soldier of the cross places full dependence, hope, and trust in God and His sovereign will above all; calls out for the Lord's help and acknowledges their weakness and sin before Him; operates by the Holy Spirit and rely upon His wisdom through revelation and illumination; and asks God to teach them His way that they might live by truth, giving them an undivided mind to revere His name (Psalm 86:11). With this mindset, the soldier of the cross is able to wage war as our Commander intends, not in a fleshly way, since the weapons of our warfare are not carnal but mighty through God for the pulling down of strongholds (2 Corinthians 10:3–4). With the Lord's help, the soldier is empowered and able to demolish arguments and bring every thought into captivity to the obedience of Christ.

My dear soldier, be sober-minded and vigilant because your individual mettle and your own internal sinful cravings will be tested by Satan. The battle between spirit and flesh is real, and battle preparations must never cease because *"our adversary the devil, as a roaring lion, walketh about, seeking whom he may devour"* (1 Peter 5:8). Seek to understand the victory secured by Christ so your mind will become courageous and strong, prepared for the schemes of the enemy.

Lead On, O King Eternal

Lead on, O King eternal,

the day of march has come;

henceforth in fields of conquest

your tents will be our home.

Through days of preparation

your grace has made us strong;

and now, O King eternal,

we lift our battle song.

Ernest W. Shurtleff (1887)

Day 1 - Divide and Conquer

Suppose ye that I am come to give peace on
earth? I tell you, Nay; but rather division.

—Luke 12:51

Even if you are physically blind, it is obvious there is no peace
on earth and there never will be until Jesus returns to reign
from Jerusalem. Earthly peace is a lie from Satan, and to
pursue it is fruitless, which is why knowing the person of Jesus Christ is
so important. Yet many are content to never learn what God's Word says
about Jesus, and others are satisfied with developing their own spiritual
understanding of Him. Think about this: since 1776, America has never
gone ten years without being involved in a war. Additionally, there has
been a major war raging somewhere on this planet at some point during
each century for the past three thousand years. Even during Jesus's first
coming, there was no peace on earth. Ultimately, when Satan entered
the Garden of Eden, war began, and the world has been in a continuous
state of conflict ever since.

As time goes on, believers should ache for Jesus to return and bring
an end to the evil that exists on this earth; Jesus did. In Luke 12:49,
Jesus said, ***"I am come to send fire on the earth; and what will I,
if it be already kindled?"*** Jesus was ordered by His Father, and He
wanted to complete that mission. Don't miss this: Jesus was hoping the
judgment of the world would happen soon after His crucifixion, but He

also understood that only His Father knew that date. Jesus hated what sin had done to His creation and despised the sin He was witnessing in the Roman Empire and especially among His own Jewish people. Jesus was God in the flesh and was living among the sin that had infected His creation, yet He also told everyone He had a "baptism" of death to finish, and despite being surrounded by sinful humans, Jesus chose to save the world through His sacrificial atonement on the cross (John 3:16). That is love!

In Luke 12:51, Jesus states something that is often overlooked. He tells His disciples He had come to divide. Jesus... a divider? Absolutely. Jesus states, *"Suppose ye that I am come to give peace on earth? I tell you, Nay; but rather division."* Jesus came to the earth to divide people. Think about what it means to follow Jesus for a moment. First, it requires full surrender—the kind of surrender that submits to the authority of Jesus. Second, it requires separation—the kind of separation that leaves behind the sinful lifestyle of your past. Third, it might cost a person their family. In extreme cases, new followers of Christ are separated from their Muslim or Hindu families because of their new life in Christ. Finally, it requires a new lifestyle—a lifestyle that includes following Jesus and doing all things for His glory, a lifestyle that will include persecution, and a lifestyle that will be filled with conflict with the world.

The follower of Christ has peace with God, an inner peace the world can't take away, nor will it ever know. In the New Testament, *"peace"* is found in an intimate relationship with Christ. If you don't have this, you have no peace with God. Jesus was the embodiment of peace when He walked the earth because He had come to reconcile the sinful humanity with God.

If you are following Christ wholeheartedly, then you have most likely experienced division with friends, coworkers, or family. The reality is that Jesus did not come to bring peace on earth, *"but rather division."* Salvation is granted when we decide to separate from the world, decide to follow Jesus, and accept the risks of being exiled by others. Who has separated and divided you from your biblical values?

Day 2 - I Have Come

For the Son of man is come to seek and save that which was lost.

—Luke 19:10

Military operations are always executed with a clear plan, and within that plan is a specific mission statement that even the lowest-ranking soldier should know. The mission is the central purpose combined with the action to be taken and the reason it must be completed. The mission clarifies and informs the soldier about what he and his unit need to accomplish. Jesus was also on a specific mission when He arrived on earth and received His commission from His Father. He was baptized and then sent into the wilderness for forty days to battle against Satan. Following His victory, Jesus was patched up by angels and supplied with the power of the Spirit to accomplish the mission He was sent to complete. Over the next three years, Jesus strategically and divinely fulfilled His mission.

During His travels, one day, He entered Jericho and encountered a tax collector named Zaccheus. Not much is known about this man, except that he was short and he wanted to see Jesus. Zaccheus wasn't just curious; he was seeking to hear the gospel message that was being proclaimed by Jesus. Ultimately, Zaccheus and his household were saved. It's then that Jesus states His primary mission: ***"For the Son of man is come to seek and save that which was lost"*** (Luke 19:10).

While Jesus made numerous statements about who He was and what He came to do, there might not be a clearer statement made about His primary mission than Luke 19:10. Like the great leader He was, Jesus took ownership of His mission and identified Himself as the Son of Man, which is significant for three reasons. First, this is the title Jesus used for Himself more than any other, eighty-three times in the Gospels. Second, it is His messianic title that refers to His humanity, His upcoming humiliation, and His glory. Ultimately, the title **"Son of Man"** refers to the mystery of the incarnation; it refers to Jesus being both divine and human and refers to Jesus being the shepherd who has come to rescue His lost sheep.

Following His divine title as the Son of Man, Jesus states His mission: *"to seek and to save that which was lost."* Using shepherd imagery, Jesus tells Zaccheus and, ultimately, the world that He was on earth to accomplish a very specific mission: to *"seek"* those who were lost (perishing) and then *"save"* them. To translate, the entire world was lost and separated from God, and only Jesus, the Good Shepherd, could *"save"* them from perishing in hell.

Jesus had one mission, and it involved a brutal and bloody death on a Roman cross, but it didn't involve defeat. You see, unlike a military operation, Jesus's death meant victory—a victory that would accomplish His mission and secure eternal life for all who come to believe upon Him for salvation. Jesus completed a mission that no one else could do—not the government and not religious rituals. Jesus came to *"seek and save that which was lost,"* and that is exactly what He did.

Have you been found by Jesus? His blood and battered body found you two thousand years ago on a hillside in Jerusalem. Being *"lost"* could last a day, or it could last for eternity.

Day 3 - Worth the Fight

Beloved, when I gave all diligence to write unto you of the common salvation, it was needful for me to write unto you, and exhort you that ye should earnestly contend for the faith which was once delivered unto the saints.

—Jude 3

I f you have ever won a sports championship or completed any type of military training, you have exerted a tremendous amount of effort to achieve your goals. Each year prior to a particular sport's season, expert analysts predict the teams that will contend for their respective championships. Based upon off-season trades, front-office decisions, draft picks, and various other factors, analysts determine whom they believe the league's contenders will be. Nevertheless, championships are not won without opposition and adversity, and in sports or in war, there is always an opponent waiting to test the mettle of a team or unit.

The Gospel also has many opponents. From Islam to heresy (false teachings), the Gospel has been and will continue to be attacked. Jude, the half-brother of Jesus, wanted to write a letter about salvation but changed his plans once he learned of the opponents who were seeking to corrupt the Gospel. The influence of these false teachers was significant and was spiritually dangerous as teachers had already begun infiltrating the teachings of the young church. Jude wrote to the church, *"Beloved...*

it was needful for me to write unto you, and exhort you that ye should earnestly contend for the faith which was once delivered unto the saints" (Jude 3). Pay attention to the word "contend" in this verse.

Jude was doing more than drawing attention to the issue of false teachers; he was calling believers to battle. Satan had declared war against God while he was still in heaven, and now he had launched a war against the Gospel (truth). Jude uses the words "earnestly contend," meaning believers are to wage war and exert intense effort, defending the truth of the Gospel. Since the first century until the present day, false teachers, under the leadership of Satan, have attacked the integrity of the Gospel and have done everything in their power to distort the purity of the Bible. Need proof? Just do a quick search, and you will discover the thousands of religions and cults that exist, all claiming to be true. However, truth rests in Christ and His Word.

So how can a soldier of the cross *"contend for the faith?"* In order to *"contend"* for something, a person must be passionate about it. No one exerts effort and energy toward something they are not passionate about, which creates a dangerous problem in cultures where persecution is insignificant and comfort is the norm. It's similar to the athlete who loses their hunger to win and becomes sluggish about his or her training; it renders him or her unable to *"contend"* for a championship. For the soldier of the cross, contending for the faith means being filled with a passion for following Jesus and the salvation of the unsaved. To be able to *"contend"* means being equipped with the correct doctrine and truth, and that is exactly why Jude wrote this letter.

How prepared are you to *"contend for the faith"*? Do you know the basic doctrines of the Christian faith, and are you prepared to recognize heresy and false teachings? Prepare yourself now to wage war against the numerous false teachings that will corrupt and contaminate the truth of the Gospel.

Day 4 - Enemy Infiltration

For there are certain men crept in unawares, who were
before of old ordained to this condemnation, ungodly
men, turning the grace of our God into lasciviousness, and
denying the only Lord God, and our Lord Jesus Christ.

—Jude 4

During World War II, Adolf Hitler ordered his Nazi troops
to disguise themselves as British and American troops while
using captured Allied tanks to cause confusion in the rear
of the Allied lines. Hitler's objective was for his troops to issue false
orders, upset communications, and misdirect the Allied troops, causing
tremendous confusion that would ultimately lead to their defeat and
death. By the grace of God, this attack was thwarted, and the Allied
forces would go on to defeat Hitler and win the war. Infiltration tactics
that use disguise and deception have been around since Satan invaded
the Garden of Eden and manifested himself in the appearance of a
serpent (Revelation 12:9). Infiltration has multiple definitions, but it
primarily means to secretly enter with the purpose of causing damage
while remaining undetected.

Now let's go back to the first century for a moment. The church was
new and was growing fast, which meant the opposition was intensifying
by the minute as Satan was placing it firmly in his crosshairs. Jude wrote,
"For there are men crept in unawares... ungodly men, turning the

grace of our God into lasciviousness, and denying the only Lord God, and our Lord Jesus Christ" (Jude 4). With thousands of years of experience, Satan knew the most effective tactic for destroying the church was to divide it from the inside, so he decided to send false teachers who were pretending to look very real and genuine.

This verse deserves full examination. First, *"men crept in unawares... ungodly men."* Who were these ungodly men? They were false teachers attempting to change and distort the teachings of Jesus Christ and corrupt the church. They were emissaries of Satan sent to encourage believers to engage in sin and defy the grace of God. In our modern age, false teachers are still very much active. They deny the authority of scripture, preach a false gospel of prosperity, deny the deity of Jesus, invent their own holy books, encourage the justification of sinful lifestyles, and destroy the Christian witness. And like the first century, false teachers secretly continue to corrupt the church while having the appearance of godliness. Second, they were *"turning the grace of our God into lasciviousness."* The false teachers were making a mockery of God's magnificent grace by encouraging *"lasciviousness"* or behavior that was grossly immoral. Through the teachings of these false teachers, the church began indulging in shameless lifestyles. It was as if they claimed to believe in Jesus while spitting in His face. Finally, the church was *"denying the only Lord God, and our Lord Jesus Christ"* with its perverted lifestyles of immorality. Sadly, the church continues to be infiltrated by false teachers and false doctrines.

Without knowing the truth about Jesus Christ and His Word, a believer will be unable to discern the strategic infiltration of false teachers and their *"lasciviousness,"* meaning the sinful nature of the human heart will be led away by greed, lust, doubt, and the numerous other sins of the flesh.

Resolve today to devote yourself to God's Word and allow the Holy Spirit to teach you everything there is to know about Satan's infiltration tactics.

Day 5 - Truth Mockers

How that they told you there should be mockers in the last
time, who should walk after their own ungodly lusts.

—Jude 18

When American service members returned home from
the Vietnam War, many were greeted by mockers who
shouted profanities and called these veterans such vile
things, such as "baby killers" and "murderers." These mockers were
expressing their displeasure with America's involvement in the Vietnam
War by mocking returning military veterans, most of who were drafted
and had suffered tremendously during their time in combat. However,
mocking is nothing new. Mockers have been around since nearly the
beginning of human life, and you can bet they were present when Noah
was building the ark in the middle of the desert. I can only imagine
what the people were saying to Noah when they saw him building a
gigantic cargo ship. Remember, these people were so wicked that God
grieved in His heart that He had even created them (Genesis 6:6). Job
was also mocked by his friends because they wrongly believed that his
sin was causing the suffering in his life. Mockers are present now, and
yes, they will be present on this earth until Jesus returns.

Jude wrote, ***"How that they told you there should be mockers in
the last time, who should walk after their own ungodly lusts"*** (Jude
18). God the Father loves the world so much that He doesn't want

His children to be taken by surprise. You see, Jesus Himself told the disciples that mockers of the truth would rise and continually become more prominent in the church. God has left His Word to His children to warn us and to ultimately protect us. Jesus loves the church; it's His bride, yet He absolutely foresaw the apostasy that was coming and ensured the Holy Spirit inspired Jude to write *"how that they told you there should be mockers."* These mockers were scoffers who had seductively wormed their way into the church and were on a mission to lead as many nominal believers astray from the truth as possible.

Jude says this will happen *"in the last time."* We are living *"in the last time."* The *"last time"* began with Jesus's first coming and will continue until His second. Therefore, soldiers of the cross should not be caught off guard. God has warned us. Like a military unit receiving a warning order, we have been warned and have even been provided needed intelligence of the enemy's tactics. You see, there is a spiritual war raging in the invisible realm, and the Lord loves His children so much that He has equipped us with the wisdom we need to win the battle against apostasy. However, without devoted study and application of God's Word, the soldier of the cross will be unprepared and eventually rendered ineffective in service to the Lord.

Finally, Jude says these *"mockers"* will *"walk after their own ungodly lusts."* These men were fueled by their flesh and were convincing members of the church to betray truth and the church and walk with them in their lusts. Their tactics included teaching heresies, twisting scripture, and encouraging believers to return to their former *"ungodly lusts."*

Jesus doesn't need His followers to defend Him; He only expects His followers to stand firm on His Word. Will you be rendered ineffective when Satan sends his *"mockers"* to attack you?

Day 6 - Glory Denied

And the Lord said, Behold the people is one, and they have all
one language; and this they begin to do and now nothing will
be restrained from them, which they have imagined to do.

—Genesis 11:6

Every day, someone somewhere is building their own kingdom.
Throughout the course of history, kingdoms have been built,
and kingdoms have been destroyed, the majority being erased
from the annals of history. Why? Because pride fueled their desire to be
powerful and it also led to their demise. History tells the story of mighty
rulers and kingdoms that were never satisfied and continually sought to
expand through tyranny and oppression. Their pride sought to make
a name for themselves regardless of the cost. We must remember that
it was pride that caused Satan (Lucifer) to rebel in heaven, and it was
also the original sin in the Garden of Eden. The Bible details how
God humbled and destroyed various kingdoms for their rebellion and
punished them for their wicked ways. Why? Because God hates pride.

Following the great flood, Noah's great-grandson Nimrod (Genesis
10:10) took it upon himself to build a great tower in the land of Shinar
(close to Babylon, Iraq). Using brick and mortar, Nimrod and his people
began building a tower *"whose top would be in the heavens"* (Genesis
11:4). The people wanted to make a name for themselves, and they
were doing all they could to prevent from *"being scattered abroad*

over the face of the whole earth" (Genesis 11:4). Now enter pride and disobedience. The people wanted to make a name for themselves so that generations after them would give them praise. Sounds familiar? It should. Our modern world is full of people who are seeking to make a name for themselves. They want to be great, the best ever, the biggest, the wealthiest, the most popular, or the most searched on the Internet. Sometimes it's subtle, and sometimes it's not, yet the human flesh continues to worship the self and feed off individual accomplishments and titles.

When people get together to build a giant tower *"whose top would be in the heavens,"* God takes notice. Here's how scripture records His response: *"And the Lord said, Behold the people is one, and they have all one language; and this they begin to do and now nothing will be restrained from them, which they have imagined to do"* (Genesis 11:6). This verse summarizes the disobedience and the prideful actions these people were guilty of, and now God had arrived to bring their efforts at immortality to an end. With the great flood removing only three generations, civilization was still in a fragile state, and humanity needed to *"fill the earth"* as the Lord had commanded in Genesis 9:1, not gather as *"one."*

You might ask why it was disobedient to have one language for the people or why would God want to restrain them from all they could *"have imagined to do."* First, if all humanity had one language, then they would have grown too powerful and too arrogant; the same is true for doing all they could imagine. We must not forget that God is sovereign, and He already had the perfect plan for redeeming mankind: His Son Jesus on a cross. Thus, the Lord had no choice but to destroy their tower, confuse their language, and scatter them all over the earth.

When human pride goes unchecked, evil and wickedness also go unrestrained. Need proof? Go back and read what became of some of the greatest empires of the past. God denied Nimrod's glory because glory belongs only to Him. Whose glory are you seeking in your life?

Day 7 - Unbroken Promises

And I will bless them that bless thee, and curse him that curseth thee: and in thee shall all families of the earth be blessed.

—Genesis 12:3

Have you ever broken a promise? Your answer should be yes. Unfortunately, broken promises have become so common that we've almost forgotten what it feels like for someone to keep a promise. American presidents are known for their broken promises. For example, during his reelection campaign in 1964, Lyndon Johnson promised he would not send ground troops into Vietnam, yet after he was sworn into office, he sent ground troops into Vietnam. Promises are directly linked to the integrity and character a person possesses; consequently, if a person fails to keep their promises, they are labeled as untrustworthy and unreliable. A promise is a declaration that a person is going to do exactly what they said they will do.

But what about God? Does He ever break His promises? The answer is a resounding no. Paul wrote, ***"For all the promises of God in him (Jesus Christ) are yea, and in him Amen, unto the glory of God by us"*** (2 Corinthians 1:20). Pay close attention to this verse because it is powerful; all God's promises in the Old and New Testaments have been fulfilled in Jesus. Paul even adds the word "Amen" because He affirms this as an absolute truth, much like a person would shout Amen during a worship service.

Ultimately, the promises of God are so rock-solid that you or I can bet our lives on them. God is faithful, and His promises, like His love, never fail.

In Genesis 12, God chooses Abraham and makes him some incredible promises. Following His promise to make Abraham into a great nation, the Lord spoke these words: ***"And I will bless them that bless thee, and curse him that curseth thee: and in thee shall all families of the earth be blessed"*** (Genesis 12:3). Abraham believed these promises from God, and he followed his belief with action. He packed up his family and all their possessions and left his comfortable home for a land he did not know. The bottom line was that Abraham obeyed God in faith, and the Lord fulfilled these promises.

God says, ***"I will bless them that bless thee, and curse him that curseth thee."*** To understand this verse, *them* and *thee* must be defined. The ***"them"*** can be divided into two categories—the nation of Israel and the church—and the Lord has and will fulfill His promises to both groups because both groups are chosen by Him. The ***"thee"*** is Abraham. The ***"him"*** is anyone who stands against the nation of Israel and rejects Jesus Christ as the savior. Jesus, as the savior of the world, descended from Israel.

Finally, God says, ***"And in thee shall all families of the earth be blessed,"*** meaning every person, whether gentile or Jew, from every nation on this earth, can be blessed through a descendant of Abraham, Jesus Christ. Paul wrote that those who are of faith (faith in Jesus Christ) are sons of Abraham (Galatians 3:7), and he also clarified that through Jesus Christ, gentile believers are grafted into the line of Abraham. In summary, God preached the Gospel to Abraham (Galatians 3:8) and then kept that promise when His Son went to the cross. All families (people) will be blessed through Abraham's descendant when they receive the finished work of Jesus Christ and repent. They will receive the blessing of eternal life.

Abraham was in heaven when God fulfilled the promises of Genesis 12, yet he believed when the Lord promised him on earth. Believing in God's promises is founded upon faith, meaning we don't need to see in order to believe. Do you believe in the unbroken promises of God? God never makes a promise He doesn't intend to keep.

Day 8 - Victory Proclaimed

And I will put enmity between thee and the woman
and between thy seed and her seed; it shall bruise
thy head, and thou shalt bruise his heel.

—Genesis 3:15

When someone guarantees victory, we often respond with doubt and skepticism. Even when an opponent is exceptionally stronger and more talented, there is still no guarantee of victory. One such astonishing victory occurred in 1948. On the same day the British pulled down their flag and Israel raised its flag, the Arab nations launched an overwhelming attack against a newly formed Israel. The odds were overwhelming—six hundred fifty thousand Jews versus forty million Arabs. There was virtually no one in the world who believed Israel would emerge victorious. We're talking about seven different armies against an initial army of thirty thousand Jews who had no organized military or command structure. In fact, Israel was only able to provide one rifle for every four soldiers. Thus, with the overwhelming military might of the Arab nations, they should have annihilated Israel. You see, Israel was vulnerable, and they were surrounded by enemy nations who wanted them wiped off the face of the earth. However, a miracle occurred, and God gave Israel victory over their enemies. When God guarantees victory, it's a sure thing.

Did you know that God guaranteed Satan's defeat in the Garden of Eden? That nearly four thousand years before Jesus arrived on earth, God proclaimed complete victory over Satan? He did. This truth alone should leave you in wonder and awe. In Genesis 3, following the fall of mankind and the arrival of sin on earth, God speaks to Satan (the serpent) and foretells of His future victory over him: *"And I will put enmity between thee and the woman and between thy seed and her seed; it shall bruise thy head, and thou shalt bruise his heel"* (Genesis 3:15).

This verse is the first hint of the Gospel, the good news that Jesus would defeat Satan and set humanity free from sin. God tells the Devil, *"I will put enmity between thee and the woman and between thy seed and her seed,"* meaning God put hatred and hostility between Eve and Satan, and not just Eve but "her future seed," Jesus Christ. Eve's *"seed"* represents not only Jesus but also all who have ever come to believe in Him. Satan's *"seed"* represents all unbelievers who willingly or unwillingly follow him (John 8:44). In summary, spiritual hostility exists between the followers of Christ and Satan.

Finally, God tells Satan, *"It shall bruise thy head, and thou shalt bruise his heel."* The *"it"* is referring to Jesus. Most translations use the word "He," but the KJV uses "it." Nevertheless, a powerful proclamation is stated here. Jesus would *"bruise thy head"* of Satan on the cross, and He will ultimately throw him into the abyss at the end of the great tribulation (Revelation 20:10). However, Satan would also *"bruise his heel,"* the heel of Jesus, meaning Satan would inflict suffering upon Jesus while He was in Roman custody and, later on, the cross. Nevertheless, Satan suffered an ultimate and definitive defeat when Jesus rose from the grave and will be finished off at Jesus's Second Coming.

Since our risen Christ ascended into heaven, each generation has battled Satan and will continue to war against the flesh. Nevertheless, are you advancing in the confidence of the Gospel? Are you confident of Jesus's full victory over Satan? Do you believe that **"the God of peace will crush Satan under your feet"** (Romans 16:20)?

Day 9 - The Final Word

Hath in these last days spoken unto us by his Son, whom He hath appointed all things, by whom also he made the worlds.

—Hebrews 1:2

Before the days of social media, satellite television, or the Internet, an important message was often communicated through an envoy or messenger who represented a leader. The leader would notify his envoy, and the envoy would then notify the people. This is essentially how God communicated with His messengers. You see, since the beginning of time, God spoke directly to either a leader or a prophet chosen by Him, who would then communicate the His message to the people. For a period of nearly 1,800 years, over thirty-nine different Old Testament books and throughout various historical settings, God spoke to individual leaders and prophets. When God wanted the world and His people to know something, He would speak to a prophet who would communicate that message. The author of Hebrews wrote that long ago, God spoke to the prophets in various times and in many ways (Hebrews 1:1). Everything you read in the Old Testament from Genesis to Malachi was communicated by God to the writer. For example, Moses received everything that transpired in the book of Genesis directly from the Lord. Moses wasn't even alive, yet the Lord communicated everything to Moses, most likely during the forty years of Israel's wanderings in the wilderness.

Following the death of Malachi, God went silent for almost four hundred years and was no longer speaking to Israel or the world for that matter. Then when the fullness of time came, God sent His Son Jesus into the world (Galatians 4:4), and the way He spoke to the world changed forever. So now *"in these last days (the Lord) has spoken unto us by his Son, whom He hath appointed all things, by whom also he made the worlds"* (Hebrews 1:2).

First, the *"last days"* began with the birth of the church and are the days in which we are living now; thus, Jesus's message of salvation and redemption has been *"spoken unto us"* and is found in the Bible for all to read. The Holy Spirit arrived to indwell believers (Acts 2:4); it was the guiding force that inspired the authors of all twenty-seven New Testament letters and continues to be the empowering source for every modern-day soldier of the cross.

Second, *"He hath appointed all things, by whom also he made the worlds."* All authority in heaven and on earth has been given to Jesus (Matthew 28:18). Don't miss this: the world and this universe have been given to Jesus because God worked through Jesus to create the universe (Colossians 1:16). Thus, Jesus is the Creator, He is the truth, and anyone seeking to know what God is like or what God has to say needs to listen to the words of Jesus. Moses spoke about Jesus, the prophets spoke about Jesus, and the Lord has spoken to us as Jesus. God has appointed Jesus as the heir of His estate—an estate that begins in heaven and encompasses the entire universe.

The truth of Hebrews 1:2 requires faith—faith that is compelled by action. This knowledge means nothing if it's not mixed with faith. God has spoken His final Word through Jesus, and the next time He speaks will be through Jesus when He arrives to reign on this earth during His Second Coming. Ultimately, Jesus is the fulfillment of everything God revealed through the centuries. Now do you believe that *"the Lord has spoken unto us by his Son"*?

Day 10 - Taste of Death

But we see Jesus, who was made a little lower than the angels
for the suffering of death, crowned with glory and honor; that
he by the grace of God should taste death for every man.

—Hebrews 2:9

The mission was at hand, the time had arrived, and under the direction of His Father, Jesus left heaven (John 6:38) and entered the earth to accomplish the most important and essential mission the world has known or ever will know. He would enter as a baby and would grow into the God-man. Jesus was the exact representation of the nature and essence of God in time and space (Hebrews 1:3), and by the time He turned thirty years of age, Jesus was prepared to make the final push toward redemption and victory over sin and Satan. Under the authority of His Father, Jesus was about to do the will of His Father who sent Him (John 6:38).

The author of Hebrews wrote, *"But we see Jesus, who was made a little lower than the angels for the suffering of death, crowned with glory and honor; that he by the grace of God should taste death for every man"* (Hebrews 2:9). This verse screams love, humility, and sacrifice but so does the entire life of Jesus. There was only one course of action, and it was a plan initiated by God before the creation of the world, which is another discussion in itself; nonetheless, it speaks to the sovereignty and supremacy of God. In order for God's plan of salvation to satisfy His wrath and fulfill the prophecies of the coming Messiah, Jesus *"was made a little lower than the angels for the suffering of death."* In simple terms, Jesus had to become a man and suffer a bloody, sacrificial death on a Roman cross to atone for the sins of humanity. The mystery is that Jesus was fully God and fully man and would operate as God on earth while under the authority of the Father in heaven. Amazing! Where Adam failed, Jesus succeeded.

Jesus was also *"crowned with glory and honor."* Jesus was perfect and without sin and was the fullness of God walking the earth. He was crowned as God's glory and given the honor as His divine representative during His time on earth—a crown that continues forever. Jesus's mission on earth was centered on the will and glory of God, and He would accomplish that mission perfectly. From His birth to His death, Jesus was only concerned about glorifying and honoring His Father, and only He was able to represent heaven and earth; thus, He was *"crowned with glory and honor."*

Finally, *"by the grace of God, Jesus tasted death for every man"* (emphasis mine). Eternal death and the wrath of God can be avoided because Jesus *"tasted death for every man."* That is the good news of the Gospel message. Without God's unimaginable grace, no one would ever be saved. God showed indescribable grace by giving His Son to satisfy His divine wrath. You see, Jesus tasted a bitter, shameful, painful, and humiliating death; was crowned with glory and honor; fulfilled God's law and the messianic prophecies of the Old Testament; and finally made redemption (set free from slavery to sin) possible for everyone who would come to believe upon His work on the cross and resurrection.

Do you believe that Jesus tasted death for you and everyone? Has your belief led you to a life of holiness and righteousness? Do confession and repentance define your life? In a culture of "easy believism" and sinners' prayers, ensure your salvation is founded upon a belief that has led to change and spiritual action.

Day 11 - Mission Complete

But this man, after he had offered one sacrifice for
sins forever, sat down at the right hand of God.

—Hebrews 10:12

For thousands of years, the Israelites would offer the same
animal sacrifices over and over, hoping to have their sins
forgiven (which were offered according to the law); yet the
blood of bulls and goats could never take away their sins (Hebrews
10:4). The law was simply a shadow of things to come, and come
"He" did. Since Cain and Abel, people have sought to earn God's
favor through outward religious actions and rituals. Think about all
the religious rituals that currently exist, some of which have been
commanded by the Lord, such as baptism and communion. However,
through the desire of people to earn God's favor and, in many cases,
earn their salvation, outward religious actions have deceived them
into believing they can please God with their actions and earn a place
in heaven. Even in my denomination, people are often confused and
believe their baptism or the raising of their hand at an evangelistic
event has secured their salvation. Religious cults believe salvation is
not a gift granted by God's grace but a way for them to work toward
their salvation through personal merit, and there are literally hundreds
of examples like these that have been invented by people. However,
rest assured that salvation is secure, redemption has been achieved,

and victory has been declared. Jesus overcame sin because humanity never could, and it's also a mission no human effort or might could ever attain.

The reality is that every type of sacrifice and religious ritual have failed to perfect mankind and satisfy the wrath of God, *"but this man (Jesus), after he had offered one sacrifice for sins forever, sat down at the right hand of God"* (Hebrews 10:12). The Lord demanded a perfect sacrifice, a blameless sacrifice, a spotless sacrifice, a sacrifice whose blood was pure and undefiled; and only Jesus could be this sacrifice and accomplish this mission of human salvation. The sacrifices offered since the beginning of time and especially the sacrifices offered by the Jews under the law were unable to forgive sin forever and ultimately take away their sins. These continual Jewish offerings were essentially nothing more than ritual purifications offered until Jesus arrived to finish the job. Don't miss this: the scripture reads, *"After he (Jesus) had offered one sacrifice for sins forever."* Jesus's one sacrifice completed the mission His Father sent Him to accomplish. It does not need to be repeated or duplicated, nor should anyone ever doubt the superiority or sufficiency of Jesus's final and perfect sacrifice. It is finished (John 19:30)! Upon taking His last breath, Jesus affirmed that His *"one sacrifice"* completed the work His Father had sent Him to accomplish.

Finally, Jesus *"sat down at the right hand of God"* like a gold medalist at the Olympics stepping onto the podium to claim his prize of victory. Jesus (back) down" with His Father in triumph. He destroyed Satan's hold on humanity and made it possible for men and women to dwell with Him forever in paradise. He left heaven, and now He had returned with complete victory in hand and offers His followers direct access to the throne of God.

Do you believe that your sins have been covered, or do you believe that your sins have been completely removed? There is a significant difference here. Are you still asking the Lord to forgive you over and over, or do you confess your sins understanding Jesus's *"one sacrifice"* forgave your sins when you first believed in His finished work on the cross? Forgiveness is a one-time action;

however, confession lasts a lifetime. If you genuinely believe in Jesus and have repented your sins, then ***"offer up a sacrifice of praise"*** (Hebrews 13:15) and thank Jesus over and over for what He did for you on the cross.

Day 12 - Gaining Life in Death

For to me to live is Christ, to die is gain.

—Philippians 1:21

Abiding in Christ enables a believer to reveal Christ in their life. As Jesus revealed His Father, believers are to reveal Jesus; they are to spiritually die so their old life can be hidden in Christ (Colossians 3:3). When we look into a mirror, it never reveals what's inside, and it can never read between the lines; yet when the eyes of the heart are opened and the perception of the mind is enlightened by the Gospel and glorious riches of Christ, a person is able to see themselves as they truly are. They are able to see every sin that dwells in their heart and examine themselves without prejudice. This is a gift the Lord gives to those whom He has regenerated by His Word and Spirit.

Ask yourself this question: how hopeful would you be if you were on house arrest or locked up in prison? Without hope in something eternal, you and I would eventually drift into despair and depression. When Paul wrote his letter to the Philippians, he was on house arrest in Rome, languishing in a cold dungeon, and chained like a common criminal. However, it provided him the perfect environment to write one of greatest letters in the Bible. You see, the Lord uses adversity and suffering to draw a person's mind and heart to His, and this is what occurred as Paul sat in prison, reflecting on how the Lord had transformed his life when they met on the road to Damascus. As a result of his bold witness for Christ, in cooperation with the Holy Spirit, Paul had found himself inside of a cold prison cell where he had come to understand what life and death were all about.

In Philippians 1:21, Paul writes that *"for to me to live is Christ, to die is gain."* What an incredible statement about Paul's view of life. In fact, it's the only view of life and death for a follower of Christ. Through submission and surrender to the will of God and by the power of the Holy Spirit, Paul was being conformed into the likeness of Jesus, and he desired to be with Him. You see, the carnal mind believes life on earth is all there is; thus, the desire for wealth, recognition, and pleasure become the most important things in life. A temporal perspective pursues self-gratification, not wanting their worldly life to end, while the eternal perspective desires the life to come and dwelling with Christ. For Paul, *"to live is Christ."* To translate, his life was Christ. The glory of Christ was his highest objective and his ultimate mission. Simply put, Paul could not imagine living without Christ, not for Christ, and not through Christ. His life was hidden in Christ and considered his previous life as garbage (Philippians 3:8).

Lastly, Paul believed *"to die is gain."* Paul believed death to be a present and eternal gain. Consequently, for the carnally minded person, death is a great loss. However, for the believer, death is the greatest gain they could ever hope for as the pain and misery of this life come to an end and the desire to be with Christ makes the departure from earth so desirable. So whether a believer lives or dies, great gain awaits, and it's a believer's faith in Jesus that allows them to see death as a gain.

If you are not ready to die, then you are not ready to live for Christ. Think about it. Eternity is where believers will ultimately and finally dwell with Christ, but we first must die physically so we can be ushered into His presence. Has your mind embraced death as a gain?

Day 13 - Humility Above All

†

Let nothing be done through strife or vainglory; but in lowliness
of mind let each esteem others better than themselves.

—Philippians 2:3

Church history is littered with disunity and strife. That is simply the unfortunate truth behind organized religion. As much as I love the church, the reality is, disunity has existed since the first century. The church has never been immune to strife or some form of dissension. Everything from murder, sexual molestation, adultery, pornography, and greed continues to wreak havoc on local churches, rendering them ineffective for the kingdom; yet the church (the regenerated believers of the Gospel) is still God's instrument on earth. In every situation of church strife, sin—or more specifically, selfish ambition—was the root cause. Whether in a family or in a church body, internal unity is essential for restraining the destructive forces that hinder the advancement of the Gospel.

The church suffered greatly during its first years of existence. The preaching of the Gospel was outlawed, church property was confiscated, Christians were fed to the lions and burned at the stake, and the Jews were constantly hunting them like animals. Some things never change; Christians are still being persecuted and crucified on crosses, church buildings are still being burned down, and the Gospel is still forbidden in dozens of Muslim countries. It's with a background of collective and individual suffering that Paul wrote to the church at Philippi. One of the primary purposes of his letter was spiritual unity as he exhorted the Philippians to love one another and be one in the Spirit. Like a good soldier, Paul had suffered for the Gospel, and he had also suffered for the sake of their unity.

After exhorting the Philippians to be of the same mind, united in spirit, and intent on one purpose, Paul writes, *"Let nothing be done through strife or vainglory; but in lowliness of mind let each esteem others better than themselves"* (Philippians 2:3). The first thing you will notice about this verse is that Paul is addressing the works of the flesh; Paul is addressing sin as we all must do in our own lives. *"Strife or vainglory"* is rooted in the flesh; this sin begins inward and manifests itself outwardly causing division in every part of our lives. Other names for *"strife"* include rivalry, conceit, and selfish ambition. All these words are words of opposition and seek individual glory instead of collective unity and the glory of God. Paul said, *"Let nothing be done through strife,"* meaning if the church of Philippi or any other body of believers are to be united, humility—not strife—will be the attitude by which they interact with one another. Strife represents partisanship and pride, and it ultimately dishonors God and steals His glory and creates tension within His church.

Lastly, *"in lowliness of mind let each esteem others better than themselves."* Let me make this simple: Christians are to be humble people. *"Lowliness of mind"* means elevating others above oneself in humility and having the same mind as Jesus. Jesus made Himself of *"no reputation,"* and so should we. The church consists of diverse individuals who are called to put others first and individuals who are called to serve God and one another. Jesus said, *"I am meek and lowly in heart"* (Matthew 11:29). Are you?

Are you walking in the same spirit as Jesus, or are you causing strife in your church or family through selfish ambition? Jesus was the perfect example of humility and lowliness. Follow Him.

Day 14 - Emptied of Self

But made himself of no reputation and took upon him the
form of a servant, and was made in the likeness of men.

—Philippians 2:7

A person's reputation is imperative; it's essential to our earthly lives. The *Merriam-Webster Dictionary* defines "reputation" as the common opinion people have about someone or something. It further defines it as the overall quality or character as seen or judged by people in general. We all consider a person's or company's reputation. We consider the reputation of those whom our children hang out with, whom our children will date and marry, the manufacturers of the products we buy, and we should consider a candidate's reputation when voting in political elections. The bottom line is that a person's actions and words either strengthen their reputation or tarnish it. Yet one of Satan's tactics is to blind the minds of unbelievers to the truth (2 Corinthians 4:4), leaving the people of the world unable to discern a person's true reputation and incapable of choosing God's reputation over their own.

The soldier of the cross imitates and follows Jesus who, during His years on earth, was hated and considered a blasphemer and law breaker by the Jews, His own people. Nevertheless, Paul wrote to the Philippians, who had never met Jesus, and exhorted them to be like Him. He told them of the humility that Jesus possessed and how He willingly emptied Himself by becoming human for their salvation. Paul told these Philippians that Jesus *"existed in the form of God"* (Philippians 2:6), that Jesus was the very nature of God, and that Jesus was equal to God. In one verse of the scripture, Paul confirmed that God dwelt among the people in the flesh of His Son and that Jesus was absolutely equal to God. In fact, the Greek word *equal* used by Paul in verse 6 means the exact same size, quantity, character, and number. Jesus was God!

Then in Philippians 2:7, Paul writes that Jesus *"made himself of no reputation and took upon him the form of a servant, and was made in the likeness of men."* This is an astounding, supernatural scripture that should leave you in awe. Jesus came to earth in perfect humility, first as a helpless infant and later in *"the form of a servant."* Jesus was equal to God, yet He *"made himself of no reputation."* Jesus voluntarily submitted *"himself"* to the authority of His Father and confined Himself to a human body, yet He never lost His divine power. Jesus *"made himself of no reputation,"* meaning He was sacrificially preparing to pour Himself out as a drink offering and save the world from eternal death (those who believe upon the Gospel). That requires a man with *"no reputation."* It requires Jesus saying, "Father, I accept Your mission of saving and redeeming the people of the world, despite the fact they don't deserve it. I accept Your mission Father to save and redeem the world despite the fact they will hate Me and kill Me, and finally, Father, I will go to earth and defeat Satan on his turf and overcome the power of death."

Jesus's whole life was a life of humiliation, callousness, poverty, and shame; He had nowhere to lay His head, was misunderstood, was a man of sorrows, was well-acquainted with grief, did not appear with external pageantry or any marks of distinction from other men. Ultimately, Jesus died the death of a slave. That is what God did for you.

Jesus emptied Himself for your sake; internalize this, and you will discover what being in Christ is all about. Whose reputation is more important in your life—yours or the Lord's?

Day 15 - Remain Calm

Take therefore no thought for morrow; for the
morrow shall take thought for the things of itself.
Sufficient unto the day is the evil thereof.

—Matthew 6:34

I n 1939, in preparation for World War II, the British government,
in their attempt to calm the fears and boost the morale of their
people, created a poster that read "Keep Calm and Carry On."
The intent was to unite and strengthen the citizens of Great Britain in
case the country came under attack; they didn't want their people to
worry or become fearful about the uncertainty of war and the future of
the country. Ironically, the signs were never distributed or displayed, yet
after a decision to conserve paper, the posters remained in storage until
the year 2000, and now this little-known slogan has become famously
printed on T-shirts all around the world. Yet can a person genuinely
Keep Calm and Carry On in their own strength? needs to be asked.
The answer is no. The flesh is weak, the flesh is fearful, and the flesh
is self-serving.

You see, Jesus also instructed His followers to "keep calm and carry
on," yet He did so apart from the human motivation of temporal safety
and survival. During His Sermon on the Mount, Jesus instructed His
disciples to ***take therefore no thought for morrow; for the morrow
shall take thought for the things of itself. Sufficient unto the day***

is the evil thereof" (Matthew 6:34). Think for a moment of all the uncertainties of life, the stress of worrying about future events, and the inability we have to prevent so much of what happens in our lives. When Jesus commanded His soldiers to *"take therefore no thought for morrow,"* He was saying, "Do not worry," or as the first-century Greek-speaking Hebrew would have understood it, "Don't tear yourself apart from the inside." The word "worry" means to tear apart or divide from the inside. Understand this: Jesus knows everything about the human body, and He absolutely understands the damage worry causes our earthly bodies because it produces stress. Stress causes almost 60 percent of all physical illnesses. The damage of stress begins inside the body, slowly weakening our immune system and making us susceptible to a variety of damaging diseases, such as heart disease. It eventually shows evidence in our face as wrinkles and bags form under the eyes, wreaking havoc inside of our earthly tents.

Should we plan aspects of our lives? Of course. Should we use discernment about upcoming events? Absolutely, however, *"for the morrow shall take thought for the things of itself."* If you have a concern or are troubled about an issue in life, you must understand God's grace is sufficient. Each day will bring its own problems, and worry changes nothing. It makes you feel worse and draws you away from God. A follower of Christ is supplied with an ample supply of God's love and mercy as they fully depend upon the Lord for their future security. For the soldier who is walking in the center of the God's will, there is nothing to worry about. The truth of the matter is that worry is a sin; it demonstrates no faith in the Lord and leads the heart to see the world greater than the Lord's sovereignty.

Finally, Jesus says, *"Sufficient unto the day is the evil thereof."* This world is already dark and broken enough since each day contains a sufficient amount of evil of its own; thus, when followers worry about tomorrow, they increase their stress and bring a degree of torment upon themselves. No matter what troubles come into your life, seek first the Lord's kingdom and His righteousness (Matthew 6:33), and the needs of this life will be given to you until the Lord calls you home.

If worrying is a problem for you, understand you are sinning before the Lord, which renders you ineffective for His kingdom. The worries of life will divide your heart and develop a lack of trust in the Lord. You can't afford either; this life is short, and the days are evil. Abide in the Lord, and take control of the worry that seeks to invade your mind. It's the only chance you have at remaining calm.

Day 16 - Retaliatory Love

But I say unto you, that ye resist not evil: but whosoever shall smite thee on thy right cheek, turn to him the other also.

—Matthew 5:39

Retaliation comes very natural to almost every human being. The natural mind desires revenge and retribution. We want to right our wrongs and ensure people or organizations are paid back for what they have done to us. No matter a person's cultural background, the sinful nature of the human heart is the same. The heart is deceitful (Jeremiah 17:9); thus, it is naturally inclined to seek reprisal. Despite personal efforts and religions, humanity remains sinful and retaliatory because the human heart was diseased and polluted by the spiritual carnage that occurred in Eden. Satan gained control of the world and sought to capitalize upon the sinfulness of the human heart. As a result, he has developed destructive schemes and tactics that have fueled and continued to fuel the wickedness of the human heart. Playing off his knowledge of the human heart, Satan desires for humanity to retaliate against one another when conflict and disagreements occur.

However, Jesus turned the human response of retaliation upside down. You see, when Jesus began His ministry on earth, He commanded His followers not to retaliate against one another, a command which He would model in His own life. Jesus spoke to challenge and train those would become His disciples, and His training was completely different than that of the world system. During Jesus's Sermon on the Mount, He addressed how His believers were to respond to evil and prevent further violence. In Matthew 5:39, Jesus said, *"But I say unto you, that ye resist not evil: but whosoever shall smite thee on thy right cheek, turn to him the other also."* This is a challenging command because it goes against everything that our flesh desires. However, may we not forgot it's the Holy Spirit that restrains evil and it's the Holy Spirit that enables us to act in response to evil in a godly manner.

Jesus stated, *"that ye resist not evil."* This is essentially impossible apart from Christ, yet it begs the question, "Why shouldn't a follower of Christ resist an evil person?" First, revenge and wrath belong to God. Second, in this context, resisting means to stand against or to oppose; thus, Jesus is saying His followers must not be revengeful people. Nonetheless, resisting evil doesn't mean we shouldn't avoid it. It means we shouldn't contemplate retaliation; it means we should go beyond the world's standards and forgive the evil person.

Finally, Jesus commands that *"whosoever shall smite thee on thy right cheek, turn to him the other also."* Jesus expects His followers to forgive those who wrong them instead of seeking revenge. The world seeks revenge, but believers seek reconciliation. In reality, there may not be a more difficult command in all scriptures than turning the other cheek. Even with the empowerment of the Holy Spirit, the flesh craves revenge. It's simply not natural to forgive someone when we have the opportunity to retaliate, which is why it's supernatural. It comes from God, and it comes from knowing Christ and walking in the Spirit.

As Jesus loved and prayed for those who cursed Him on the cross, we are to love and pray for those who have hurt us. While believers have the right to defend themselves, we must use godly discernment before we act upon our anger and understand we are citizens of heaven.

Are you giving mercy to those who wrong you, or are you expecting to receive it? Christ, like love, retaliates by showing love and forgiveness when those who have wronged us don't deserve it. That is what the grace of Gospel illuminates.

Day 17 - Rescue Mission

And she will bring forth a son, and thou shalt call his name JESUS: for shall save his people from their sins.

—Matthew 1:21

We all love a story where someone is saved from the grip of death. It makes us feel good inside and motivates our spirits. Toward the end of World War II, US forces breached the gates of Dachau concentration camp in Germany, and before their eyes were thousands of starving prisoners, many near death. The American soldiers also came across the gruesome discovery of thirty railroad cars piled high with Jewish bodies. From its establishment in 1933 until the camp was liberated in 1945, more than 188,000 prisoners passed through the heavy gates of Dachau. At least twenty-eight thousand people died within its walls, although the exact number who lost their lives under its regime will never likely be known. What these Jewish prisoners needed was a savior, so God sent American forces across the ocean to liberate them and set them free. However, while God intervened to eventually save the Jews from their German captors, their liberation would be no different from their ancestor's deliverance from Egypt or the countless pagan groups who threatened their existence in the ancient past. This liberation, like all the other liberations, was only temporary.

The greatest need of humanity is to be rescued from its sin, and this required a supernatural plan that only the Creator of humanity could set into motion. It's a plan that was foreordained before for the foundation of the world (1 Peter 1:20), and when all the events that needed to occur on earth had been completed (Galatians 4:4), God was ready to send His Son into the earth. To announce this extraordinary message of good news, the Lord sent the angel Gabriel to earth to notify Mary and her husband Joseph. It was during a dream that Gabriel appeared to Joseph and spoke these words: *"and she will bring forth a son, and thou shalt call his name JESUS: for shall save his people from their sins"* (Matthew 1:21).

The time had finally arrived for the Savior to enter time and space, and Joseph was undoubtedly confounded with the news that the Holy Spirit had conceived Jesus inside of his virgin fiancée. God had chosen his future wife to *"bring forth"* the Son of God and had chosen him to be his earthly father, and they would have no choice in the child's name; His name would be Jesus. When Joseph heard that name, he knew it meant "the Lord shall save" since it was a common Jewish name. Furthermore, the name "Jesus" specifically expressed the redemptive work He would accomplish during His time on earth. Ultimately, Gabriel provided Joseph his son's mission as well. Jesus was to *"save his people from their sins."*

This rescue mission had been announced in the Garden of Eden, and now it was launched inside of the womb of Mary. The baby King would be born from a virgin, apart from the sinful seed of man, so He could rescue *"his people from their sins"* and save them from eternal death in hell. While not fully understanding the gravity of Gabriel's statement, Joseph obeyed and took Mary as his wife, so he could provide the physical care Jesus would need as a young child.

Have you been rescued from your sins, or are you still imprisoned inside of the walls of Satan's concentration camp? Jesus has the key to let you out, and He stands ready to grant you eternal life. His birth represents an eternal mission to rescue you from hell, and only your lack of belief and repentance can thwart your rescue.

Day 18 - Unstoppable

For verily I say unto you, Till heaven and earth pass, one jot or one tittle shall in no wise pass from the law, till all be fulfilled.

—Matthew 5:18

G od's Word is unstoppable and eternal. Let me explain. First, the Word can refer to both the Bible and Jesus Christ. The Bible has always been referred to as God's Word because it is the written form of God's Word. For example, the phrase *"thus says the Lord"* occurs over four hundred times in the Old Testament. You see, when God spoke to His prophets and shepherd leaders, His words were recorded on whatever form of writing material they possessed and were preserved into what we now call the Bible. The written Word of God was sustained by God so generations could come to know Him and provide the prophetic proof necessary to confirm the existence of His Son Jesus before the foundations of the world, and nothing is going to thwart God's Word. Since antiquity, Satan has tried to destroy the Bible; the Babylonians burned down the temple where the Old Testament scrolls were kept, the Roman Emperors tried to destroy it, even the Roman Catholic Church burned thousands of copies during the middle ages, and more recently, a French atheist named Voltaire falsely predicted that within one hundred years, the Bible and Christianity would be swept from existence and into oblivion. All these efforts by the enemy failed because God's Word is unstoppable.

The prophet Isaiah wrote, *"The grass withers; the flower fades, but the word of our God stands forever"* (Isaiah 40:8). God's word tells of His divine plan for the universe and for mankind, and it is permanent. It's not like grass or flowers that fade and wither; it stands through all attacks and persecution because it's supernatural and not of this world. Furthermore, Jesus, the living word, said this about the written word: *"For verily I say unto you, Till heaven and earth pass, one jot or one tittle shall in no wise pass from the law, till all be fulfilled"* (Matthew 5:18). You see, earth and heaven will pass away, everything you see will pass away, but the Word of the Lord will endure forever. Everything written by God, to include the law, which has already been fulfilled in Christ; the prophecies of the Old Testament, which will be completely fulfilled in the millennium reign of Christ and with the coming of the New Jerusalem; and the Gospel which has been revealed in Christ are unstoppable.

When Jesus says *"verily,"* He means truth or, say, "This is how it is, and this is how it will be." Jesus refers to *"heaven and earth"* to express the unchangeable nature of God's word compared to the temporal state of this earth. He then states that "*one jot or one title shall in no wise pass from the law.*" A rabbi or a scribe would understand this perfectly since each letter and stroke of the pen was divinely significant when new copies were made. Thus, nothing written in the Old Testament (and later the New Testament) would be forgotten about until it is fulfilled.

The Lord is unchanging, and His Word is unstoppable; it's the most sure thing in the universe. Do you take God at His Word? Your salvation depends on it.

Day 19 - Living Faith

For unto us was the gospel preached, as well as unto
them: but the word preached did not profit them, not
being mixed with faith in them that heard it.

—Hebrews 4:2

Y ou could attend church services every Sunday, read the Bible
every day, even travel back in time and listen to the apostle
Paul preach the Gospel; however, unless you mix what you
hear with faith, it will be useless. Reading the Bible cannot save you,
knowing the Bible cannot save you, going to church cannot save you,
understanding the Gospel cannot save you, nor will those achievements
make you a better person. The Israelites knew the scriptures, but they
still died in the wilderness separated from God. Why? Because the
Israelites failed to mix their knowledge of the law with genuine faith.
You see, faith is the key to experiencing God and all that He has
promised in the Bible. The author of Hebrews wrote, *"For unto us was
the gospel preached, as well as unto them: but the word preached
did not profit them, not being mixed with faith in them that heard
it."* If the Gospel is to save your soul, it must be mixed and received
with genuine faith.

Hebrews 11:1 defines "faith" as both *"substance"* and *"evidence."*
"Substance" is the matter of which something is built. For example,
in Hebrews 1:3, the author tells us that Jesus is the *"radiance of His*

glory and the exact representation of His nature." The Greek word used for *"nature"* is the same word used in the definition of faith in Hebrews 11:1 as *"substance."* In other words, what this verse is saying is that God became visible. He became a substance in Jesus Christ. Jesus Christ is the substance of faith; He was God in human form, and just as Jesus is the substance of God who invisible, faith is the substance of those things that we hope for that are invisible. Evidence is the second part of the Hebrews 11:1 definition. Evidence is what we look for in a substance to determine whether it is genuine and true. In fact, your faith is evidence; your faith determines the outcome of what you believe, yet it is based on the invisible because the scripture that states *"believe on the Lord Jesus Christ, and you will be saved"* (Acts 16:31) goes beyond the natural or what we can see and defies our ability to use logic.

So how can your faith in Jesus be living and real? First, your faith must see God for who He is and believe in every promise written in the Bible. Through faith, you can see beyond your circumstances and your man-made solutions and believe that Jesus, who is invisible and dwells in heaven, is in control and that only He can do the impossible. Second and most importantly, your faith is not given to you to get whatever you want in this life; it given to bring you what God wants for you. Third, you must stop walking by sight. Sight is opposed to faith, and if you walk by sight, there is no room for faith to work in your life. You must remember that your old nature (the flesh) desires to see everything before acting, but your new nature is able to believe without seeing or feeling because that new nature comes directly from God.

Faith is not something you utilize when someone is sick or when you run out of money. Every moment of life is to be lived in faith. If you want the promises of God to have power in your life, you must believe in God's Word and His sovereign will for your life.

"Faith" is a noun, but "believe" is a verb, meaning it indicates action. Has your faith in Christ led you to a life of obedience? If not, perhaps it has never been fixed with genuine faith.

Day 20 - Choose Life

I have set before you life and death, blessing and cursing:
therefore choose life; that both thou and thy seed may live.

—Deuteronomy 30:19

L ove will forever be defined by God choosing the world through His Son on a bloody cross. In fact, that bloody cross represents the ultimate symbol of love and the greatest act of love the world has ever known. Nevertheless, it will remain the most hated symbol in the world until the Lord returns for His millennial reign. Our human minds cannot begin to fully comprehend how the Lord chose to save believers before the foundation of the world (Ephesians 1:4). The most important and costly decision a person can make in this life is the decision to believe upon the Gospel and surrender to Jesus. Every day, men, women, and children choose to follow Jesus, gain eternal life, and accept the cost of becoming a Christian in a Muslim nation or another land that is hostile to believers in Christ. Why? Because only the one true God offers "life" through His Son Jesus. There is no guarantee of comfort, no guarantee of riches, no guarantee of good health, and no guarantee of physical safety. Only that the soul of a follower of Christ is secure for eternity and that they will receive a crown of righteousness that is incorruptible.

As Jesus invites people to choose "eternal life" through Him, Moses exhorted the Israelites to choose life on the plains of Moab. The Israelites were camped across from the Promise Land, and they could literally see the land God had promised them. The forty years of wandering in the wilderness were over, and the Lord was about to fulfill the covenant He had promised Abraham and his descendants. A journey that should have taken eleven days was now concluding after forty years of death and punishment. It was now time for God's chosen people to choose between life and death, and thus it was time for Moses to demand a decision by stating, *"I have set before you life and death, blessing and cursing: therefore choose life; that both thou and thy seed may live"* (Deuteronomy 30:19). To translate, to obey God meant life; to disobey God meant death. The choice was before the Israelites; they knew the law, and they had seen firsthand the miracles of the Red Sea and the manna. It was now decision time.

Nearly 1,400 years after the death of Moses, the choice of life and death is still before the people of the earth. However, this choice is made possible by the grace of God, not by the law of God. It's a choice with eternal consequences and earthly persecution. It's a choice that will bring about internal peace or spiritual instability. It's a choice that will justify a person in the eyes of God or condemn them into eternal hell. The good news (the Gospel) is that the Holy Spirit (the third person of the Trinity) is still at work, bringing conviction of sin and offering full reconciliation with the Creator of all life. Ultimately, only Jesus offers an escape from eternal death, unconditional forgiveness, and a new life. The path of eternal life and salvation is clear and pure, it's written about in the pages of the Bible, and it's so straightforward that even the simplest mind can understand it.

While Moses no longer calls us to life, *"the One Moses wrote about in the Law"* (John 1:45) does—Jesus Christ. The terms of eternal life require genuine belief and understanding in the finished work of Jesus Christ. May we never forget that the primary duty of the soldier of the Cross is to love God and to love Him as the Lord.

Day 21 - Distress Call

And Samuel took a sucking lamb, and offered it for a
burnt offering wholly unto the LORD: and Samuel cried
unto the LORD for Israel; and the LORD heard him.

—1 Samuel 7:9

For hundreds of years, people aboard ships have used distress signals and calls to announce they were in imminent danger that could potentially lead to the loss of life. Signals—such as flares, white flags, sirens, smoke, and other types of calls—have been used to declare lives were at risk. When God created man in His image, He gave them the ability to communicate with Him, both verbally and nonverbally. Man has the moral sensibilities and intellectual abilities to know God and to call out to Him in distress or, most importantly, for repentance and salvation. Calling God to act and intercede is a privilege and an honor for the soldier of the cross. The Lord listens and responds appropriately not only for His glory primarily but also for our spiritual benefit as well.

The prophet Samuel's chief responsibility was to speak the truth and communicate God's commands to the people of Israel. Following the Philistine's capture of the ark of the covenant, Israel had fallen into great distress. For His glory and in anger, the Lord punished the Philistines for capturing His ark by throwing them into confusion and inflicted them with tumors, resulting in the death of many. The ark was eventually returned to Israel, yet Israel was still in need of deliverance from the Philistines and desperately needed to return to the Lord as a nation. Samuel pleaded with Israel to *"return to the Lord with all their heart and remove the foreign Gods from among them"* (1 Samuel 7:3), and they did. Thus, after acting faithfully and obediently to Samuel's demand, Israel cried out to Samuel to intercede for them with God: *"And Samuel took a sucking lamb, and offered it for a burnt offering wholly unto the LORD: and Samuel cried unto the LORD for Israel; and the LORD heard him"* (1 Samuel 7:9).

As believers, we should be able to identify with Israel. We still possess a corrupt nature; it's called our flesh, which inclines us to see ourselves as worthy when in actuality, we are unworthy of any relief from God. We still struggle with the same sins that Israel did; we fail to forsake the world and, in return, become carnal-minded. Samuel's intention was pure, and the people of Israel knew it. His prayer was not empty; he brought a sacrifice that was offered purely for the glory of God. Ultimately, Samuel brought the perfect ingredients for prayer. He brought his faith, his sacrifice, his tears, and a deep reliance and love for the Lord.

As soldiers of the cross, we no longer need to bring a *"sucking lamb"* because the Lamb of God has already been offered on a bloody cross. The Lord heard the distress calls of the people before the foundation of the universe and set in motion a plan to lay bare His Son Jesus before the same people whom Samuel offered the *"sucking lamb."* However, unlike Samuel, Jesus prayed and interceded for the world while nailed to a Roman cross. Even as Samuel offered the lamb before the Lord, it wasn't the sacrifice the Lord was looking at; it was the motive and intent of Samuel's heart.

Our flesh is corrupt, and with it, our desires depraved. It's through our regeneration and the abandonment of our natural man that puts us in a state of grace. Our minds must be set on the grace and mercy of the Lord if we are to intercede like Samuel and experience the riches of Christ. A day of failing to become more like Christ is indeed a day of distress.

Day 22 - God Strong

✝

We then that are strong ought to bear the infirmities
of the weak, and not to please ourselves.

—Romans 15:1

Teams consist of a mixture of people; some are weak, and some are strong. Some are considered starters, and some are considered bench players. Nonetheless, anyone who has ever been part of a team loves a teammate who is selfless, a teammate who is willing to sacrifice his body and individual achievement for the success of the team. Oftentimes, these selfless teammates are the strongest members of a team as they have the ability to deny themselves so the team can become stronger and receive the glory. The Lord also expects His soldiers who are the strongest in their faith to help those who are the weakest. This is what the church is about; unfortunately, the ratio of strong to weak might be more out of balance than ever before.

When Paul was writing his letter to the Romans, he spoke about the need of believers to bear the weakness of others, to assist weaker believers, and to cover their limitations. However, the possibility of this requires a servant's mind-set—a mind-set devoid of self while seeking the welfare of those who are weak. In Romans 15:1, Paul wrote, **"We then that are strong ought to bear the infirmities of the weak, and not to please ourselves."** We each have weaknesses, whether we are weak or strong in the Lord. Yet this is the beauty of the body of Christ at work—many members supporting and bearing with one another. In the verses prior to chapter 15, Paul wrote about the conscience of a believer and how those who are strong can cause those who are weak to stumble in their spiritual growth, stating that spiritual strengths should either be kept private or used to build up weaker believers.

So what is Paul exhorting the spiritually strong to do? First, they must *"bear the infirmities of the weak."* Simply put, the strong are to *"bear"* or support those who are weak in their faith. We have brothers and sisters in Christ who are weak; thus, they are called to *"bear,"* not like a post serves as the bearing point for a structural beam but as a servant who comes alongside with the understanding of a weaker brother or sister's conscience. As new creations in Christ, concern for others now supersedes our former selfish nature to please ourselves. In the world, the strong tend to walk over the weak as they build their personal empires. Nevertheless, like Gen. Christopher Gadsden coined the phrase "Don't tread on me" during the Revolutionary War, followers of Christ are to stand with weaker believers and ensure they don't allow their religious freedom to tread on the consciences of the weak. Second, after surrendering our lives to Christ, the strengths we possess are viewed from a new perspective, an eternal perspective. Our spiritual strengths are to bring glory to the Lord and to edify others as we continue to mature. A soldier of the cross is to move forward helping other believers grow in their maturity while never hindering their spiritual growth.

Finally, we are no longer living *"to please ourselves."* Our old nature lives to please the self, it exists to elevate the self, and it ultimately seeks to rob the Lord of the glory He deserves. What God commands is for His chosen to please Him by placing the needs of the weak above their own. Like a military soldier sacrifices to protect the weak from tyranny and oppression, believers serve to deny self while *"bearing"* with the weak until they are strong. *"Defend the weak and the fatherless; uphold the cause of the poor and the oppressed"* (Psalm 82:3). May this prayer from Asaph become an outflowing of the Holy Spirit in your life.

Day 23 - Continual Evil

And God saw that the wickedness of man was great
in the earth, and that every imagination of the
thoughts of his heart was only evil continually.

—Genesis 6:5

Human depravity caused by original sin has slowly and radically eroded the human mind and amplified the physical ailments of the human body. The original sin that dwells inside of man becomes the fuel for Satan's schemes until man humbles himself before Christ, believes upon the Gospel, and is filled with the Spirit. Then and only then can a person be rescued from the grip of Satan and be set free from the full wrath their sin deserves. The effects of original sin are such that man cannot see the error of his way; he is blinded and dead in his trespasses. An unredeemed man is like a soldier marching into battle, oblivious to the tactics of his enemy. Ultimately, man cannot see that he is lost, and the most destructive of all, without the Holy Spirit, Satan continues to draw the sinner through his world system until no part of a person's being is under the control of Satan. Is anything beyond the evil of original sin? The answer is no. From the sin that is unseen by the human eye to the worst terrorists acts that have ever occurred on this planet, nothing should surprise the follower of Christ who understands the depravity of human sin.

There is perhaps no other verse in the Bible more telling of human wickedness than Genesis 6:5 that states, *"And God saw that the wickedness of man was great in the earth, and that every imagination of the thoughts of his heart was only evil continually."* The Lord was grieved in His heart with how depraved humanity had become. He wasn't surprised, but He was pained that His creation had fallen so far from the perfection that existed in the Garden of Eden. The evil of original sin was deliberate, and God found nothing good inside of man. The first part of this verse states, *"that God saw."* What did God see? He saw everything—their imaginations, the deepest thoughts of their hearts, their emotions, their habits, and their wanton disregard for Him. As God incarnate, Jesus could also see what was inside of man (John 2:25) and was equally grieved by what He saw, and may we not forget that He was with God when He pronounced judgment on the earth in the days of Noah. Ultimately, God sees and knows everything about man because He has complete and unlimited knowledge of everything in the universe, even the deepest thoughts of a person's mind.

Second, *"the wickedness of man was great in the earth."* The scriptures don't provide all the details of just how wicked the world had become. However, we know that paradise had been lost (Adam and Eve were banished from the Garden of Eden), murder had occurred (Cain killed Abel), and the mightiest men on earth were the wickedest as they intermarried with whomever they chose and engaged in sexual perversion (Genesis 6:4). Nonetheless, the fountain of sin that flowed from their imaginations was so heinous that God regretted He had made man on the earth (Genesis 6:6). What is invisible to us is clear and magnified to our Creator. God is the one who searches and knows our hearts (Psalm 139:23).

Finally, let us be reminded daily that we deserve hell and were powerless to be saved from that dreadful destination. Our greatest strength is knowing that we are weak and have been rescued from eternal death by grace. Our enemy is still on this earth, and original sin still dwells inside of each of us; thus, the Spirit who inspired the scriptures will expect obedience to the scriptures.

Day 24 - Conclusion

✝

Let us hear the conclusion of the whole matter: Fear God, and keep his commandments; for this is the whole duty of man.

—Ecclesiastes 12:13

Life on earth is important, but it will pass like a fleeting shadow (Psalms 144:4). Just ask any person over eighty years of age, and they will tell you how their life has been but a breath. Our Lord, knowing how quickly earthly life passes compared to eternity, exhorted His followers to set their minds on things from above not on the things of this earth (Colossians 3:2). Unfortunately, our minds become consumed with the complexities of this life, drawing us into a world where everything seems more important than seeking the Lord. You see, our human minds are unable to explain this world; sin has complicated everything it has touched, from government to personal relationships, making it difficult to discover genuine happiness.

At the end of his life, King Solomon reflected on the principles he had learned. In the book of Ecclesiastes, Solomon endeavors to answer some of life's most difficult questions. Now at the end of his life, "the preacher Solomon" found everything apart from pursuing God as "vanity." He writes, *"Let us hear the conclusion of the whole matter: Fear God, and keep his commandments; for this is the whole duty of man"* (Ecclesiastes 12:13). When a man is old and his life is behind him, he is able to see the vanity of every pursuit apart from knowing the Lord.

This was the position and mind-set from which Solomon wrote. His life was coming to an end, and every pleasure he had ever enjoyed and all the riches he was granted were "all vanity," and he finally understood that all mankind would face the same physical death.

First, Solomon wants each person to *"hear the conclusion of the whole matter,"* and that conclusion is that nothing in this life is worth pursuing as a means of happiness, except that which God has ordained for us and the quest of knowing Him. Second, Solomon has discovered to *"fear God and to keep his commandments."* There is not a more worthy pursuit than living in the fear of the Lord with a deep reverence for His holiness and giving Him the honor due His majesty. A genuine soldier of Christ possesses an inward and outward reverence for His gospel that compels them to worship Him in truth while surrendering their rights to His will. It's through the commandments and the whole of God's Word that we come to "fear" the Lord. Where reverence exists, duty exists; where reverence reigns, a love for righteousness reigns. Can a person truly keep His commandments? No, but Jesus Christ has, and what is His is now ours. The empowerment of the Holy Spirit provides the believer's conscience the conviction to keep the commandments close and to love them. The commandments represent the heart of God and the standards by which He demands His people to measure themselves. By falling short, we are able to visualize the expanse between our weaknesses and Christ's strength and to visualize His worthiness and our unworthiness.

A good soldier fulfills their duty, and for the soldier of Christ, their *"whole duty"* begins at the cross and ends at glorification. Our *"whole duty"* in this life is to *"fear the Lord and keep his commandments."* It's in the performance of this duty that we are able to learn His will, discover how Jesus accomplished this, and continually honor Him with our lives.

Day 25 - Genuine Repentance

I will arise and go to my father, and will say unto him,
Father; I have sinned against heaven, and before thee.

—Luke 15:18

homas Watson wrote, "Sin must first be seen before it can be wept for." Sin demands judgment because it's intolerable in the sight of God. Sin, which has its origin in heaven, required the blood of our Lord to satisfy the wrath it rightly deserves. Repentance is the acknowledgment that we are at risk of perishing into eternal flames because of the sin that dwells inside of us, transferred by the blood of Adam. Repentance is realized through the power and light of the Gospel. The Gospel illuminates the sin nature that dwells inside of humanity, which gloriously brings the understanding and inward desire to repent.

Jesus stated, *"Joy shall be in heaven over one sinner that repenteth, more than over ninety and nine just persons"* (Luke 15:7). Repentance is pleasing in the sight of God because it fills the air of heaven with a sweet-smelling aroma. Genuine repentance demonstrates to God a heart that is willing to submit to His Son Christ and humble themselves before His holiness. In the parable of the prodigal son, we learn of a father's son who sinfully squanders his inheritance through wayward living. It's a parable that symbolizes God as the common Creator and Father of all mankind. It's a parable that tells the story of a son who has rebelled against his father's goodness and love and a father who has willingly allowed his son to do what is right in his own eyes, despite the consequences. It's a parable of a son who distanced himself from his father, and ultimately, it's a story of grace and repentance.

Once the prodigal son *"came to himself"* (Luke 15:17), meaning he returned to his right mind, understood his sinful state, and was disgusted by what it had cost him. It's then that he said within himself, *"I will arise and go to my father, and will say unto him, Father; I have sinned against heaven, and before thee"* (Luke 15:18). As the old saying goes, before a person can come to Christ, they must first come to himself as the prodigal did. The consequences of the prodigal's sin had brought him to a state of brokenness and the absolute decision to *"arise and go to his father"* and seek forgiveness and reconciliation. There was to be no delay; his first act upon awakening was to go to his father.

The prodigal had most importantly judged and condemned himself. He understood that he was not even worthy to be called a son (Luke 15:19). His heart was filled with sorrow as he understood how he had *"sinned against heaven and before thee."* Following the genuine repentance of the prodigal we see the beauty and grace of the father. We see the contrast between what it's like to be lost and what it's like to been found. We see grace.

In summary, the prodigal parable brings to light the readiness of the Heavenly Father to forgive the poor in spirit and celebrate their decision. The father of the prodigal son is the representation of God the Father who is willing to embrace a repentant sinner who has grown tired of their sinful state and is ready to turn to Jesus Christ for a new life. The Lord is rich in mercy to those who have seen their unworthiness in the Gospel message. Have you?

Day 26 - Wise Men Seek Him

✝

Where is he that is born King of the Jews? for we have seen
his star in the east, and are come to worship him.

—Matthew 2:2

One of the great mysteries of God is how He directs people to accomplish His will. Throughout the Bible, we read account after account of God directing the events of history and, ultimately, the actions of men and women. When the Lord decides it's time for an event to be fulfilled, He moves people to action, often against the understanding of the people involved. In fact, there are numerous promises of God directing people, especially those who belong to Him. For example, King David wrote of God's direction that *"the steps of a good man are ordered by the LORD"* (Psalm 37:23) and *"I will guide thee with mine eye"* (Psalm 32:8). God's prevailing purpose for the world cannot be stopped. No matter who a person is or where they are from, God, by His sovereign power, will ensure affairs that impact eternity are accomplished.

One of the more miraculous affairs in history is how the Lord guided some pagan wise men (magi) to visit Jesus after His birth. These men obviously had knowledge of the scriptures that foretold of Jesus's coming since they had arrived in Jerusalem, looking to worship Him after his birth in Bethlehem. How did they find Jesus? God placed a supernatural star in the sky for these wise men, who were astrologers, to be guided. While many questions remain why no one else was able to see this star or why the Lord chose to only reveal it to them, the fact remains that God provided these men with divine revelation and illumination so they could make their way to Jerusalem and worship the Christ child. Additionally, their arrival in Jerusalem set into motion the fulfillment of messianic prophecies relating to Jesus's flight into Egypt.

When the wise men arrived in Jerusalem, they began asking around town, *"Where is he that is born King of the Jews? for we have seen his star in the east, and are come to worship him"* (Matthew 2:2). They didn't ask whether Jesus had been born; they were asking where King Jesus was. The Lord had already confirmed His birth to them, and they had just traveled nearly one thousand miles to *"worship him"*; thus, they were like soldiers on a mission, asking, *"Where is he that is born King of the Jews?"* Jesus was born a King, and these wise men knew it and, accordingly, were willing to walk and ride on a camel over dangerous terrains at tremendous risks to their own lives to worship Him.

Finally, the wise men identified how they were guided to Jerusalem and their ultimate objective: *"For we have seen his star in the east, and are come to worship him."* These men were led by God using a special star that He placed in the sky to specifically identify Jesus's location and were on a divine mission to find the One the prophets of old had spoken about. This was a supernatural mission orchestrated by God, influenced by the Holy Spirit, and took them to the Word that had recently became flesh—Jesus Christ. Had they come to truly worship Jesus? Well, they had come to worship Him but not as their Lord or their Savior.

The significance of the wise men's journey and pursuit of Jesus tells a story of unstoppable desire and divine influence converging to kneel before Jesus. While the wise men traveled close to one thousand miles to reach the feet of Jesus, many will travel down every wide path of life until they find the narrow path that will take them to Christ, to a genuine understanding of their sin, and to their desperate need for His gospel. As Jesus waited for His Father to send these wise men to worship Him, He still awaits for *"wise men"* to seek Him and kneel before Him, broken over their sins.

Day 27 - False Prosperity

Bring ye all the tithes into the storehouse, that there may
be meat in mine house, and prove me herewith.

—Malachi 3:10

The Bible is a book of multiple covenants between God,
different individuals (Adam, Noah, Abraham, and David),
the nation of Israel, and ultimately, the church. It is a book
divided by an old covenant and a new covenant. An old covenant is based
upon continual animal sacrifices, messianic prophecies, and complete
fulfillment found in Jesus Christ through His perfect obedience, His
sacrificial death, and His Second Coming. In fact, the law was a shadow
of the good things to come since the blood of bulls and goats couldn't
take away sins (Hebrew 10:1, 4). It is through Christ that the moral,
ceremonial, and judicial law has been satisfied in God's eyes. Thus, if
the law of God has found fulfillment in Christ, it begs the question:
which laws are to be carried forward into the life of the follower of
Christ?

One such law that has been carried over into the church is tithing.
The first time we see the word "tithe" in the Bible is prior to the law
as Abram offers Melchizedek (the priest of God) a tenth of the spoils
he had collected from his battles (Genesis 14:20). It's a tithe based
upon the respect Abram had toward Melchizedek as the priest of God
and an amount he believed he owed God for the victory granted to

him in battle. Ultimately, this tithe was a tithe of thankfulness. Later when the law was given to Moses, tithing became essential to support the Tabernacle, the Levites, and the nation of Israel. However, God didn't ask for their money; He asked for their produce, their crops, and their animals (Leviticus 27:30–32). In modern times, tithing finds its origins from the Catholic Church and then carried forward through the protestant reformation.

While this devotion is not a comprehensive detailing of tithing for the soldier of the cross, it is my intent to expound upon Malachi 3:10, which has been grossly misinterpreted by most Christians and used by pastors to coerce members to give 10 percent of their income. Speaking through Malachi, God commands the people of Israel to ***"bring ye all the tithes into the storehouse, that there may be meat in mine house, and prove me herewith"*** (Malachi 3:10). Thus, the soldier of the cross, with a continual objective to understand and obey the orders of their commander (Jesus), needs to value scriptures involving stewardship and giving.

The background behind this verse is how the returned exiles and, more importantly, the priests of God had departed from His law to include withholding their tithes and taxes from the new temple and the Levites. In the end, the people of Israel were robbing God and hurting the recently reestablished theocracy. The Lord, in His mercy, commanded His people to repent and ***"bring ye all the tithes into the storehouse."*** To translate, He commanded His people to repent of their sinful actions, pay their taxes and tithes, and fill the storehouse of the temple so it can be maintained and the Levites could continue their ministry. The storehouse was a large room in or attached to the temple where the agricultural offerings were stored. It was also referred to as the temple treasury. Secondly, it was important ***"there be meat in mine house."*** Simply put, this was the food and subsistence by which the Levites lived upon. This was like the basic allowance for subsistence (BAS) provided to every service member in the armed forces. Finally, the Lord asked them to ***"prove me therewith."*** This was God asking His people to try Him and see if He would keep His promise to bless them as the law had stated.

In the end, Malachi 3:10 was specifically directed at the Israelites and was never meant to be a promise of financial prosperity to individual Christians. Love and generosity are to fill the storehouse in every believer's heart as no guarantee of prosperity has ever been promised in the new covenant of Christ.

Day 28 - Never Shrink Back

For I have not shunned to declare unto you all the counsel of God.

—Acts 20:27

Courage is rare. In fact, it's so uncommon it has become difficult to identify in modern civilization. It has been redefined by our postmodern culture as taking a stand to live an immoral lifestyle, all while winning the praise of the world. Genuine courage always derives from the empowerment of the Holy Spirit as His supernatural power compels a soldier of the cross to accomplish objectives otherwise impossible. The Bible is filled with individuals who have achieved feats of extraordinary and incredible bravery because God empowered them with the courage necessary for mission completion.

In the book of Acts, the apostle Paul demonstrates courage the modern-day soldier of the cross can scarcely comprehend. He faced persecution the majority of believers will never know, and he did so with godly courage and boldness that only came through the power of knowing Christ and His Spirit. What was Paul's mind-set about the future and his earthly life? When the prophet Agabus told Paul by the inspiration of the Holy Spirit that he would be delivered into the hands of the Romans by the Jews, Paul responded; *"I am ready not only to be bound, but also to die in Jerusalem for the name of the Lord Jesus"* (Acts 21:13).

While Paul was addressing the Ephesian church leadership, he spoke in town after town of how he faced affliction and chains and how he counted his life of no value to himself so that he may finish his course for Christ (Acts 20:23–24). It was godly courage that compelled Paul to state, *"For I have not shunned to declare unto you all the counsel of God"* (Acts 20:27). Some translations read, *"I did not shrink back."* Paul was full of courage, and nothing in the world was going to prevent Him from accomplishing his mission for God *"to testify the gospel of God's grace"* (Acts 20:24). Like a soldier under the authority of a courageous and competent military commander, Paul drew from the inspiration of Christ, knowing circumstances or the schemes of Satan would not be able to ultimately obstruct him from his duty. Paul knew that proclaiming the pure and undefiled Gospel was dangerous and would provoke the anger of the Jews going forward in his ministry. In fact, he had already experienced the wrath of the Jews and their hatred for the Gospel, yet he never *"shunned to declare"* the good news that brings eternal life.

Finally, Paul's courage enabled him to declare fully *"all the counsel of God."* The greatest obstacle for a soldier of the cross is fear. Fear doesn't come from God but from Satan as it infects the soul like a debilitating virus that works to weaken and strip a person of their courage. Courageously, Paul proclaimed the full *"counsel of God,"* meaning God's entire plan of salvation from the fall of humanity through the complete work of Jesus Christ and His resurrection. Paul spoke these words to encourage the church leadership in Ephesus because he foresaw the opposition Satan would send against them. Even today, believers remain fearful to declare the full *"counsel of God"* because of the risk to life or personal well-being. Paul was faithful to never compromise the truth of the Gospel (God's plan for human salvation), and it was the Holy Spirit supplied courage that permitted him to do so.

Follow the example of Paul and our Lord Jesus, and never shrink back from courageously proclaiming the full counsel of God the Gospel demands.

Day 29 - Required Submission

Likewise, ye wives, be in subjection to your own husbands;
that, if any obey not the word, they also may without
the word be won by the conversation of the wives.

—1 Peter 3:1

Marriage is God's plan for human procreation, companionship, family stability, the discipleship of children, and perhaps most importantly, the instrument to maintain order in a fallen world. God demands order within His creation and established that by uniting Adam and Eve as husband and wife and placing Adam in charge of creation (Genesis 2:15). The scripture specifically tells of how the Lord saw a need for Adam to have a companion and states that *"it is not good that the man should be alone; I will make him an help meet for him"* (Genesis 2:18). Adam's life was incomplete, and he needed a helper. Thus, the Lord provided him a wife as a necessity and out of compassion for his loneliness.

From the beginning of creation, the concept of submission was established as the animals submitted to Adam's rule and Adam submitted to God. As God's representative on earth, Adam was given dominion over the earth, and then the woman was created from his rib to be his helpmate. However, in modern times, the idea of submission has become controversial, especially of wives toward their husbands as divorce and increasing cohabitation have tarnished the institution of marriage. Other sinful factors—such as homosexual civil unions, twentieth-century feminism, and failure of men to lead their homes—have eroded the principal of godly submission.

In Peter's first letter, he wrote to exhort believers on how they should respond to the persecution they were experiencing and call them to holy living as a means of providing a strong Christian witness to those living among them, and marriage was a powerful means for this to be accomplished. Following Peter's commands to Christian slaves, he states, *"Likewise, ye wives, be in subjection to your own husbands; that, if any obey not the word, they also may without the word be won by the conversation of the wives"* (1 Peter 3:1). Strong families create a strong community, and the foundation of the family is a husband and wife submitted to the lordship of Jesus Christ and His gospel and a wife submitted to a godly husband. Thus, Peter is saying to wives *"likewise"* as slaves do and submit to their husbands as this will bring *"favor with God"* (1 Peter 2:20).

Peter is commanding wives to be *"in subjection to their own husbands."* Is Peter commanding wives to be slaves to their husbands? Absolutely not! In fact, Peter affirmed the equality of men and women; however, he emphasized their distinctive roles. As submission to Christ brings Him glory, so does submission to appropriate authorities in society and in the home, which is why Peter courageously commanded wives to submit to their husbands. If there is order and submission in the home, there will be better order in civilization. The headship of the husband in the home is further confirmed by Paul when he wrote, *"For the husband is the head of the wife"* (Ephesians 5:23). Finally, Peter says that wives should submit to their husbands even if their husbands *"obey not the word"* and they should do so *"without the word,"* and this could possibly lead to them *"being won by their conversation."* To translate, wives possess a tremendous opportunity and witness to win their husbands and many others to Christ through godly submission and conduct.

Ultimately, a wife's submission symbolizes Jesus's submission to His Father's will to offer Himself up to satisfy the wrath demanded for human sin. Nothing testifies of love more than godly submission and obedience.

Day 30 - Knowing Eternal Life

And this is life eternal, that they might know thee the only
true God, and Jesus Christ, whom thou hast sent.

—John 17:3

There is sweetness to the sound of the words "eternal life."
They are words that ring with anticipation and heavenly
desire. For a genuine follower of Christ, there is an emotional
exhilaration at the thought of eternal life, and perhaps nothing brings
more joy to the human soul than to meditate upon everlasting life with
Jesus. To know God is to sample eternal life, and knowing Jesus Christ
allows a soldier of the cross to know God. Thus, eternal life is directly
centered on Jesus. It's centered on the Gospel message, and everything
God has promised in His Holy Scriptures. In effect, eternal life came
about through God's love for His hopeless creation. It's the beginning
and the end of human thought, and it's the hope that propels us forward
in the darkest times.

In the Gospel of John, Jesus *"looked up to heaven"* and said these words: *"and
this is life eternal, that they might know thee the only true God, and Jesus Christ,
whom thou hast sent"* (John 17:3). These powerful words are part of Jesus's prayer
to His Father when His hour of sacrifice had come. He begins His prayer by giving
thanks to His Father for giving Him authority over all flesh in order to grant those
who had and would believe in Him eternal life. As great leaders do, Jesus provides
the blessed end state to His soldiers—an end state that is not defined by physical
death but which can be enjoyed spiritually while on earth.

Jesus essentially defines eternal life by stating *"and this is life eternal."* How does Jesus define *"life eternal"*? By telling His followers that eternal life lies in the knowledge of God through Him, meaning His followers can enjoy the benefits of eternal life on earth by possessing a believing knowledge of the Gospel, of God, and of Himself. It means that those who have intimate knowledge of Jesus Christ will, by a small measure, be able to experience what eternal life is while living on earth as they dwell in communion with God and abide in Christ. Jesus prayed and told the world that eternal life was granted on earth so *"that they might know thee the only true God, and Jesus Christ."* Jesus loves His followers so much that He grants them heavenly and intimate knowledge through His indwelling presence and the almighty written word. That is love!

This verse concludes with Jesus confirming that God had sent Him with the specific mission of saving the world and granting eternal life when he prays *"whom thou hast sent."* God sent His Son as there was no other hope for mankind's eternity. When the fullness of time came, God sent His son to redeem mankind (Galatians 4:4). Jesus would become the mediator between mankind and God, granting those who acknowledge His Lordship direct access, leading to *"life eternal."*

To *"know thee only true God, and Jesus Christ"* is akin to living outside of heaven and not being able to enter. It's like seeing the glory and smelling heaven's sweet aroma but not being able to experience its fullness. Ultimately, it's the next best thing to dwelling in the physical presence of Jesus. Our Lord prepares us and allows us to taste the sweetness of knowing eternal life while on earth, before we experience genuine everlasting life with Jesus in heaven.

Are you experiencing eternal life through knowing *"thee only true God, and Jesus Christ?"*

Day 31 - Sovereignty Unveiled

Surely the Lord God will do nothing, but he revealeth
his secret unto his servants the prophets.

—Amos 3:7

The truth about love is that it keeps no secrets, and the truth about God is that He is love (1 John 4:16). In Hebrew, the word "secret" means the intimate counsel of God. Consequently, the ancient Hebrews knew that God's law revealed the most intimate counsel He could provide them, and conversely, the greatest secrets of God were found in prophecy, and the inspired knowledge He revealed to His people through His chosen prophets. One such prophet was Amos. Amos was called to proclaim God's message of judgment to the northern kingdom of Israel—a message centered on God's promises and focused on the repentance and condemnation of empty worship. Therefore, Amos was on mission for God with a singular purpose to remain faithful to the Lord in His prophetic ministry. However, it wasn't about Amos; it was about God's message of punishment and His love for His lost and sinful people.

If our lives were at risk of destruction or death, we would want someone to warn us. In fact, anything else would show a complete disregard for our well-being. Warnings are good for all people as they prevent death and serious bodily injury. Ultimately, warnings are acts of love and, in cooperation with the unveiling of God's secrets, were the primary mission of God's prophets. Amos spoke boldly to Israel and proclaimed that God's sovereignty was certain regarding their future if they continued on their sinful course. Amos spoke nothing except what the Lord wanted him to speak, and he did so in love despite the harshness of God's message. As the mouthpiece of God and as a fellow Hebrew, Amos wanted nothing more than for his own people to receive God's prophetic message with urgency and then willingly repent.

God demanded relationship and was grieved when Israel strayed and violated that covenant relationship. Amos declared his authority as God's prophet, and the Lord's willingness to reveal Israel's coming judgment by proclaiming, *"Surely the Lord God will do nothing, but he revealeth his secret unto his servants the prophets"* (Amos 3:7). The prophecy of approaching judgment is founded upon love, which is why the Lord sends this message of judgment with His chosen prophets. When Amos told the leaders of Israel that *"surely the Lord God will do nothing,"* he meant that God would never do anything as unloving as leaving His people ignorant to His divine plans for judgment. He chose His prophet (Amos in this text) and then gave them His message. Since God is love, He *"will do nothing"* without warning because His words were not only spoken to announce judgment but for reproof, correction, and righteousness (2 Timothy 3:16).

Finally, *"he revealeth his secret unto his servants the prophet."* The author of Hebrews proclaimed that God spoke at various times and in various ways to the fathers by the prophets but, in these last days, has spoken through His Son Jesus (Hebrews 1:1). Prior to Jesus walking the earth, the secrets of God were revealed to His prophets to be delivered to the world. Consequently, the people could clearly know the intimate counsel of God and His expectations of them.

If you want to know the deepest secrets of God and discover His most intimate counsel, then surrender to His will, lay the Gospel upon your heart, and dwell in the pages of the Lord's Holy Scriptures and commands.

Day 32 - Help Me, Lord

Then came she and worshipped him, saying, Lord, help me.

—Matthew 15:25

How many soldiers have cried out ***"Lord, help me"*** from the battlefields of this earth? How many soldiers have spoken these words with their final breath without ever trusting in the merits of Jesus Christ for their salvation? Only the Lord knows. The words ***"Lord, help me"*** are also the preparatory words for a person when they first understand their depravity and spiritual lostness. These are words that come from the inner most parts of a person's being when they come to the end of themselves and realize they are hopeless. They are also the words that followers of Christ speak as they learn complete dependence upon the grace and mercy of God.

There was once a Canaanite woman whose daughter was being tormented by a demon. She was a gentile who had discovered that Jesus was the Lord and the Son of David. She had heard the stories of His miracles and had come crying out for Jesus to save her daughter. Her approach to Jesus was prompted by her faith in who He was. He was the Messiah, and she knew it. The same is true today for those who call upon Jesus as Lord and Savior. Those who come to Jesus broken and drawn by the Holy Spirit are prepared to place themselves under His lordship and genuinely understand their hopelessness apart from Him and His grace. The woman in this story was no different.

When the woman first cried out, Jesus *"didn't say a word to her"* (Matthew 15:23), which most likely compelled her to cry out more. Since Jesus knew what she was thinking already, perhaps He did this to test her persistence in order to prepare her for a life of persistent prayer, which would soon go through Him as mediator and intercessor. As Jesus's disciples were about to send her away and when Jesus seemed to dismiss her as a gentile, *"then came she and worshipped him, saying, Lord, help me"* (Matthews 15:25). Some translations read that she knelt before Him. Why? Because her faith was persistent and her love for her daughter was as great.

This mother's love for her daughter is a depiction of God's love for the world (John 3:16). His love for His creation had persisted through the thousands of years of sin and rebellion until the time was right for Him to send His Son Jesus to reconcile and to redeem. Her love was unconditional and her faith drove her to the feet of Jesus, and once Jesus saw her great faith, He delighted and had compassion upon her. She had come to worship Jesus, man's chief duty on earth; and when Jesus saw her courageous faith, He could no longer deny her. She cried, *"Lord, help me,"* and the Lord responded to her faith by delivering her daughter from this demon.

Not a day should pass without the follower of Christ speaking these same words: *"Lord, help me."* We need Him, we can't live without Him, and we shouldn't move forward without His help. Are you needy and brokenhearted enough that you are crying out to Jesus, *"Lord, help me"*? This is not a one-time and done confession, although that is where salvation begins. The call of *"Lord, help me"* sustains a right relationship with Christ and forms an intimacy that provides us the solution for the most difficult and darkness moments of life.

Learn from this simple Canaanite woman and train your heart to cry out, *"Lord, help me."*

Day 33 - Get Behind Me, Satan

✝

But he turned, and said unto Peter, Get thee behind me,
Satan: thou art an offense unto me, for thou savourest not
the things that be of God, but those that be of men.

—Matthew 16:23

The will of man is dangerous, contemptible, and rebels against the Lord's divine order. The human will stand in opposition to the will of God and His sovereign plan for each person and the world. This opposition creates anxiety and a constant state of disconcertedness within the unbeliever's heart. It also creates a mind that can't rest and a life that is unsettled. It should also produce tension in the mind of the soldier of the cross. When Jesus walked the earth, He surrounded Himself with regular men who possessed a human will controlled by the original sin that dwelt inside of them. However, these men were benefiting from the greatest discipleship a believer will ever experience. For three years, their human will was being replaced with God's. They were undergoing the greatest transformation and spiritual education a human being could ever imagine; they walked with God Himself in the flesh of His Son Jesus.

What they saw and experienced is beyond comprehension. To be immersed in the seminary of Jesus was life-changing but also full of conflict. One such conflict His twelve disciples experienced was Jesus showing them that He *"would suffer many things from the elders and chief priests and the scribes, and be killed"* (Matthew 16:21). These words pierced their hearts and filled them with sorrow and disbelief. How could the Messiah be killed, much less resurrected from the dead? Their human wills could not understand it, and Peter sought to stop it. Peter had his own agenda, and it was deeply misguided and selfish, and thus he decided to rebuke Jesus. In defense of Peter, his response was natural because he loved Jesus and his understanding was limited. Nevertheless, the disciples would gain incredible knowledge and wisdom about God's divine will as a result of Peter's rebuke.

After listening to Peter's fleshly reprove and wanting to send Peter and the world a strong admonishment, the scripture reads, *"But he turned, and said unto Peter, Get thee behind me, Satan: thou art an offense unto me, for thou savourest not the things that be of God, but those that be of men"* (Matthew 16:23). Peter's intentions were selfish, and they also lacked wisdom. Was Jesus talking to Satan? No. However, Jesus answered Peter's rebuke as if He was speaking to Satan. Jesus had left heaven to offer up His life as a sacrifice for the sin of the world. His mission was to fulfill the law and willingly shed His pure and righteous blood for the atonement for sinful mankind's debt to their Creator. Peter's will stood in the way of Jesus accomplishing His mission and the divine will of His Father. Jesus came to spend Himself, not to spare Himself.

Ultimately, Peter's will was offensive, and His intentions were not mindful of God's will. Despite confessing Jesus as the Christ and the Son of the Living God (Matthew 16:16), Peter was still thinking temporal and worldly. Like a soldier engaged in combat, the follower of Christ must elevate their duty above personal ambitions if they are to successfully complete their mission and win the battle. Peter's eyes were now opened to God's will and the necessity of denying his flesh.

Who do you need to gently rebuke or perhaps remove from your life what is hindering you from obeying God's will and fulfilling your duty as a soldier of the cross?

Day 34 - Manifest Righteousness

And righteousness shall be the girdle of his loins,
and faithfulness the girdle of his reins.

—Isaiah 11:5

Equipment is absolutely essential for the soldier as he marches into battle. Despite the evolution of warfare and the advancement of weapons, a soldier still must wear the appropriate gear to keep himself protected and effective in battlefield conditions. The soldier of the cross requires a uniform that they cannot provide. It's made up of armor that only God can supply, and most notably, it's freely given to those who are indwelt by the Holy Spirit, conditional upon their genuine belief in the Gospel. It's granted to those who seek after the heart of God and the knowledge and grace found only in Christ. One such piece of armor is that of righteousness (Ephesians 6:14).

To the ancient Hebrews, "righteousness" meant walking with God and obeying His ways while He empowered them to live a morally pleasing life. They understood that God's righteousness was characterized by being perfect in all moral proportions and perfectly just in His actions. Thus, when a person walked in obedience to God's laws, they were empowered to live with integrity and righteousness.

In Isaiah's messianic prophecy about the Second Coming of Jesus, he wrote about a Messiah who would come wearing a belt of righteousness and faithfulness. Isaiah proclaimed, *"Righteousness shall be the girdle of his loins, and faithfulness the girdle of his reins"* (Isaiah 11:5). When Jesus walked the earth two thousand years ago, He became the righteousness of God (1 Corinthians 1:30) because He was God. Jesus was completely and perfectly righteous; in effect, He was manifested as righteousness in the flesh. Jesus arrived as God's living example of what righteousness looks like and awakened the world to their need for righteousness, especially the Jews who had drifted from the righteousness of God's Law. The Father made Jesus who had no sin to be sin for us so that through Him, believers might become the righteousness of God (2 Corinthians 5:21).

Conversely, when Isaiah wrote that *"righteousness shall be the girdle of his loins,"* he meant that upon Jesus's return for His millennial reign, righteousness will be His strength and will stabilize the whole world. The *"girdle"* was used by ancient Hebrews to secure their clothing and to gather up their robes so they wouldn't become loose and scatter. Thus, Isaiah is proclaiming that Jesus will govern with absolute righteousness and justice, and it will be as if righteousness is continually around Him as a girdle would be around a person.

May we not forget the faithfulness of Jesus that will be the *"girdle of his reins."* The word "reins" means the inner most parts of man. Hence, Jesus will arrive for His reign as the King of Kings as the embodiment of absolute truthfulness and faithfulness, just as He did to the suffering servant during His incarnation, only this time, He will do so as the lion. It will be unlike the world has ever known—a King who will govern with absolute righteousness and faithfulness.

Belief in the Gospel imputes the righteousness of Jesus onto the believer. Jesus's work is placed into our account. His meeting the demands of God's law is now ours, leading to our souls being justified and acceptable to God. We are made righteous because of Jesus and His work alone.

Day 35 - Tested by Fire

Every man's work shall be made manifest: for the day
shall declare it, because it shall be revealed by fire; and
fire shall try every man's work of what sort it is.

—1 Corinthians 3:13

N o one can argue the importance of a solid foundation. The
effects of using inadequate materials or building upon poor
soil conditions will eventually result in collapse or serious
structural failure. While the construction of a building's foundation
is dependent upon materials and soil conditions, a believer's spiritual
foundation is built upon the finished work of Jesus and His role as
Creator and Savior. Paul told the Corinthian believers they were
"God's building" (1 Corinthians 3:9), meaning they were standing
upon a foundation established by Jesus before the foundation of the
world, a foundation established through divine and purifying blood, a
foundation established in eternity past and one that is everlasting. While
everything else will crumble, the eternal and perpetual foundation of
Jesus Christ will stand.

After establishing that there is only one foundation that has been
laid, that of Jesus Christ (v. 11), Paul spoke of the kind of materials
(works and fruits) that should be built upon Christ's eternal foundation
and what would happen to these materials that were unworthy of His
holy standards. Paul proclaimed, **"Every man's work shall be made**

manifest: for the day shall declare it, because it shall be revealed by fire; and fire shall try every man's work of what sort it is" (1 Corinthians 3:13). Paul magnifies the imperishable nature of Jesus's foundation and exhorts all believers to take caution in what they build upon a foundation constructed upon God's own perfect blood.

"Every man's work shall be made manifest" is a reference to every believer's work being laid open for all to see and, most importantly, laid open before Jesus who already knows our works. Full light will reveal the works that the soldier of the cross has built upon the foundation that Jesus has laid. Meaning, the Lord Jesus will judge between the works that were accomplished from the flesh and the pride of man and those from the Spirit as Jesus was the manifestation of God in the flesh while on earth, so will the works of each believer as they enter the kingdom of heaven. Paul tells that the *"the day shall declare it."* The implication here is that Jesus alone will decide which works were made of gold and which were made of straw upon the day of a believer's physical death. This *"day"* will mark the end of each believer's life on earth and the end of their pilgrimage.

Finally, Paul proclaims that the works of genuine believers *"shall be revealed by fire; and fire shall try every man's work of what sort it is."* What is built upon the foundation laid by Christ Himself will be tested by Him. The master builder will test the work of His servants. As fire differentiates between gold and dross, our Lord will test our spiritual works and determine what is holy versus unholy, what is righteous versus unrighteous, what is of the Spirit versus what is of our corrupted flesh, and the standard of judgment will be His own Word and the level of knowledge each believer had of His Word.

It's the one who has confessed that they are nothing apart from the foundation, that they are unworthy apart from the worthiness of Jesus, and the one who doesn't just stand upon the foundation but has spent their life kneeling upon it, seeking the One who laid it with blood.

Day 36 - Veiled Gospel

But if our gospel be hid, it is hid to them that are lost.

—2 Corinthians 4:3

We have all tried to convince someone to believe something we feel strongly about with the goal of having them come around to our point of view, and what we discover is just how challenging and, oftentimes, impossible this can be. Many factors impact a person's belief system, such as how they were raised, who raised them, their mental illness, the geographical region in which they were raised, their culture, their political worldview, and the schemes of Satan; the factors are limitless. However, most significantly is that each person has been born under the curse of original sin because of Adam's disobedience. God's Word tells us that in Adam, all died (spiritually), so also in Christ, all will be made alive (1 Corinthians 15:22), which brings me to the Gospel—the only message that can save the lost that walk in spiritual darkness because of Adam's transgressions. We can have a lost person read the scriptures about the human curse of sin and the effects of Adam's transgressions and then show them the wonderful news of Jesus's redemptive work on the cross and His miraculous resurrection; however, unless an individual's soul is awakened by the Spirit of God to their depravity, these are mere words on a page.

In Paul's second letter to the Corinthians, he wrote, ***"But if our gospel be hid, it is hid to them that are lost"*** (2 Corinthians 4:3). This is a verse that deserves an explanation so that the correct interpretation can be derived. Why would God hide the Gospel? The answer is, He hasn't. Satan has. In verse 4, Paul informs us that the god of this age (Satan) has blinded people so they can't see and believe in the Gospel, which provides us a glimpse into the spiritual warfare a soldier of the cross must be aware of in planning their prayer strategy. The struggle for souls is intense, and it's fought against invisible foes. These foes of wickedness are the ones described by Paul in Ephesians 6:12, which is why the soldier of the cross prepares for battle through prayer and in the power of the Spirit.

According to Paul, there are two types of people: those who are perishing and those who are being saved by the Gospel (1 Corinthians 1:18). Thus, the Gospel is veiled to the wise because they view it as foolishness. Sadly, those who reject the Gospel do so because *"the god of this age"* has blinded their minds using liberal education, human wisdom, relativism, and various other tactics, placing a veil over the Gospel. *"But if our gospel be hid,"* it's hidden because of the darkness of this world brought about through the curse of man and an enemy whose mission is to keep the Gospel hidden, and this enemy will do everything within his power to continually darken the understanding of people.

If the Gospel *"is hid to them that are lost,"* it must be the soldier's mission to rescue them from their lostness. It's a mission the world doesn't understand because it doesn't require human intellect but intense prayer and the drawing power of the Holy Spirit (John 6:44). The battle against Satan is a spiritual fight that must keep us alert, watchful, and prayerful.

Let us seek the Lord for the blind who are unable to know the Gospel. Let us pray for the veil to be lifted so the light of salvation and redemption can be seen. This warfare calls us to continual duty for God's mission to cure Gospel blindness as our Lord did for the apostle Paul.

Day 37 - Darkened Hearts

They have not known nor understood: for he hath shut their eyes,
that they cannot see; and their hearts, that they cannot understand.

—Isaiah 44:18

A deceived mind is one of the most dangerous things in this
world and is also the greatest form of blindness, which is
why God has so much to say about it. There had even been
times when God commanded His prophets to preach a message that
would prevent belief in the truth. It's a timeless message from God to
those who have hardened their hearts toward repentance and belief in
the Gospel. The Lord understands the curse of this world better than
anyone, including Satan, and while He is patient and long-suffering
(Exodus 34:6), He will eventually deliver people over to the lusts of
their hearts because their foolish hearts were darkened by extensive and
wicked sin (Romans 1:21, 24). Even during conception, Jesus reveals
Himself to the parents and to the child as the Creator of all things
visible and invisible (Colossians 1:15), leaving all people without excuse.
However, since the power of darkness is real and human beings have
the free will to choose their life in respect of God's sovereignty, many
souls are led by Satan's numerous complex schemes of darkness, which
hardens individual minds toward their sinfulness and their spiritual
accountability to God.

Isaiah witnessed the final years of Israel's spiritual decline and the disaster that followed, and God was now calling him to prophesy to Judah. No matter the age, idolatry plagues every generation, and it caused devastating results upon the whole nation of Israel. Isaiah condemned and exposed the wickedness of idolatry by demonstrating how foolish it was to place trust in some man-made object compared to worshiping God himself, particularly when the idol of worship was made of the same wood they were using for cooking their food (Isaiah 44:16). Unfortunately, their idolatry had continued for so long that God had shut their eyes to the truth and allowed their hearts to become darkened. Isaiah proclaimed that *"they have not known nor understood: for he hath shut their eyes, that they cannot see; and their hearts, that they cannot understand"* (Isaiah 44:18). Is there a worse pronouncement a prophet of God could make? No, particularly if you were a Jew who no longer knew God because of your years of gross idolatry.

First, Isaiah said, *"They have not known nor understood."* Because of their extended devotion to foreign idols, Judah no longer knew or understood who God was. Don't misunderstand this; they still knew about God, yet their sinful hearts had stopped obeying the law, and their spiritual knowledge of God was all but gone. Through many years of idiotic idolatry, they had forgotten the one true God and replaced Him with idols made from stone and wood and the Lord decided to *"shut their eyes,"* meaning God delivered them over to their idols because His patience had run out. Isaiah wrote, *"They cannot see; and their hearts, that they cannot understand."* What happened to the Israelites in Judah is comparable to a student who studied to know a particular subject and then drifted away from it for a number of years. The knowledge and passion for that subject ceased as they turned away to follow something else. The Jews could no longer see their sin and their passion for obeying the law was long gone. Satan had sent them visual and man-made objects of worship.

God is commanding every soldier of the cross to identify man-made objects of worship in their lives so the wickedness of idolatry will not push Him off His throne.

Day 38 - Immeasurable Greatness

✝

And what is the exceeding greatness of his power to us-ward
who believe, according to the working of his mighty power.

—Ephesians 1:19

Can the greatness of God be measured? Not even close. It's unfathomable to our finite minds. God has revealed His greatness, continues to reveal His greatness, and will do so at the end of time through judgment and wrath that is immeasurable. The greatness of Jesus alone exceeds our understanding and draws the human heart into a deep reservoir of grace that feeds the soldier of the cross their entire life on earth. The mere definition of greatness demands close examination since it carries a range of individual meanings. However, when the word appears in the Greek scriptures, it refers to the greatness of God's power, a power firmly magnified in the second person of the Trinity, Jesus Christ. This is greatness we cannot fully appreciate, and despite the study and devotion to God, we will barely scratch the surface.

What Paul knew was that all the power of God existed in Christ, and this was a message he had been commissioned by Jesus Himself to proclaim, and it would be the "saints and believers" (Ephesians 1:1) in Ephesus whom God would choose to receive this specific message. After praying that the eyes of their hearts would be enlightened, Paul wrote, ***"And what is the exceeding greatness of his power to us-ward who***

believe, according to the working of his mighty power" (Ephesians 1:19). The depth of this truth demands examination.

First, everything about Jesus is ***"exceeding greatness,"*** meaning the greatness of Jesus is so abundant, it's beyond measure. His power, authority, and strength are conferred upon those who believe upon Him and His gospel. The soldier of the cross is fueled and equipped via the blood that flows through the exceedingly great power of Jesus. Only Jesus can offer ***"exceeding greatness,"*** and may we look nowhere or to no one else. Nothing of human flesh compares. We also must acknowledge we offer nothing great to the Lord because we have nothing great in us until He sends the Holy Spirit, which enables us to know God through the life of His Son Jesus, and even then, our original corruption battles the Spirit within us until our last breath. Lastly, take note of the direction by which God's power comes—"us-ward," or for our sake, and toward those whom He has chosen on the cross.

Finally, ***"according to the working on his mighty power."*** Paul wants the church to be aware that Jesus has completed the work necessary to bring God's power to them through His final sacrifice and resurrection. It took God's own blood to secure the salvation of His elect and the finished work of His Son Jesus to impart His great power. The helpless humanity was spiritually dead, corrupted by original sin, and was desperate for the power of their Creator. Those who have bowed a knee to Jesus and humbly proclaimed their depravity and, most importantly, the power needed to overcome their flesh and sin before Him are partakers of all His spiritual blessings.

The abundance of God's power is an everlasting spring that will never run dry; we only need to drink it in with thankfulness. Will you allow your heart to follow the cross and reflect upon the Gospel? Gospel clarity develops into a mind that realizes human weakness and frailty and requests the provision and nourishment of God's power which flows through Christ.

Day 39 - True Surety

✝

By so much was Jesus made a surety of a better testament.

—Hebrews 7:22

Certainty is something our human nature craves because it satisfies the flesh by providing the illusion we have control over our lives. Yet what we learn is that our earthly lives are riddled with uncertainty and our inability to control the sureness of future events. However, the human soul needs a foundation of certainty for inner peace to dwell within, and when the soul genuinely seeks God, it discovers this certainty in His Son Jesus who offers a covenant of surety. A "surety" is a person who promises to answer for the debt of another. For who can answer for the sin debt of another human being? Only Jesus alone.

The author of Hebrews tells how the indestructible life of Jesus became a surety to everyone who believes upon the Gospel. He tells the divine story of how Jesus was a priest in the order of Melchizedek (Hebrews 7:17), a priest who doesn't need to offer sacrifices every day but has offered Himself once and for all (Hebrews 7:27). With this in mind, the author boldly states, *"By so much was Jesus made a surety of a better testament"* (Hebrews 7:22). Jesus has conquered death and lives to intervene for those who come to understand the purpose and mystery of His blood, which are called by Him. His blood still cries from the cross, ready to offer eternal certainty to all who are drawn by the Spirit through their acknowledgment of deserving death. This certainty is made alive by a new covenant stamped in God's own blood and guaranteed by the righteousness of Jesus's flawless life.

The author is proclaiming the glory of the Gospel and of Jesus becoming a surety for all who have believed upon His life and resurrection. Jesus alone is our surety because He, being both man and God, united sinful humanity with God the Father through the assurance of full reconciliation guaranteed by His spotless and perfect sacrificial life. It took death to bring life, it took perfection to die for the sins of man once and for all, and it took divine blood to fulfill the law of God. The surety of Jesus is an everlasting promise to grant eternal life and bring the soldiers of Christ into the secure presence of their heavenly home.

Furthermore, the scripture reads that Jesus is not just a surety but *"a surety of a better testament."* If there is ever a testament (covenant) that is absolute and certain, it is the new covenant sealed in God's blood and guaranteed through Jesus's perfect righteousness, who serves as a mediator and a high priest between His followers on earth and His Father. Ultimately, the legal ramifications of Christ's atoning death declare our eternal security. By God's own law, blood had to be shed to purge sin's wicked consequences (Hebrews 9:22), and Jesus took this full responsibility upon Himself and paid the debt necessary to satisfy His Father's wrath. Now, Soldier of Christ, rest assured that Jesus has accepted legal responsibility for your sins' penalty, has forgiven them, and has paid your debt in full by the Great High Priest.

He will fulfill His promise; Jesus is our surety. He has performed His duty, He has appeared before the court, He has accepted the penalty you and I rightfully deserve, His compassion and love have won out, and grace has saved our souls. Brothers and sisters, there is certainty in Christ.

Day 40 - Peace Accomplished

Glory to God in the highest, and on earth
peace, good will toward men.

—Luke 2:14

As the Roman Empire reigned supreme upon the earth, the ancient of days, in His infinite knowledge, was about to fulfill His promise by sending forth the Messiah through a teenager. Peace in the form of a person, a baby, was being supernaturally conceived inside a virgin's womb. It was a silent night, and lowly shepherds were watching over sheep outside the sleepy town of Bethlehem, the hometown of Israel's great King David. The second person of the Trinity was taking on human flesh, becoming both God and man inside of Mary.

Long before the creation of the universe, God had prepared a merciful plan for the redemption of mankind and had predestined this time to bring forth His Son into the earth for the most important mission that has ever existed—a mission that required God's personal intervention and His almighty power. Consequently, a savior was needed with divine blood that was pure and undefiled and a savior who could bridge the immense gulf between sinful man and God. The world needed the God-man, Jesus. He didn't need the world, but as the Christ, He had love and compassion on fallen people who had rejected and disobeyed His Father since the days of Eden. Love and grace had arrived in the form of a humble baby.

On the evening of Jesus's birth, a multitude of angels assembled in a nearby pasture to proclaim His arrival to simple shepherds. The angels proclaimed, *"Glory to God in the highest, and on earth peace, good will toward men"* (Luke 2:14). Above all, they declared that Jesus's birth brought *"Glory to God in the highest."* The incarnation of God was complete; Jesus had arrived in human flesh. *"And the Word was made flesh, and dwelt among us, (and we beheld his glory, the glory as of the only begotten of the Father,) full of grace and truth"* (John 1:14). Jesus had been born into a world He had created for the purpose of being God's sacrificial lamb in order to save an undeserving world from the justifiable wrath of original sin. That is why the angels assembled to sing and proclaim, *"Glory to God in the highest."* God was showing goodwill, kindness, and love toward men who were unworthy of being saved, and He was doing it in a way that was, and still is, incomprehensible to the human mind, even to the angels.

Lastly, Jesus's divine birth brought peace on earth because the redemption of human souls made reconciliation with the Creator attainable. The reconciliation that the baby Jesus would secure as an adult made peace with God on earth possible, which humanity had not experienced since before our fall in the Garden of Eden.

The reality of Christmas is that Jesus's birth was about God extending *"good will toward men."* The giving of His Son was the beginning of God's undeserved kindness and grace toward sinful man. Delight this day that God the Father extended abundant grace toward you and I by giving us the gift of salvation and peace wrapped in human flesh. The angels were not partakers of human nature; nevertheless, they celebrated with elation at God's underserved gift of Jesus. How much more should you and I?

God's Message to Humanity – The Gospel

✝

After the prophet Nathan confronted King David about his adultery with Bathsheba, David wrote of the conviction that occurs when the human soul is persuaded of its wickedness and the conscious is made aware of its unworthiness before God. David wrote, *"Have mercy upon me, O God, according to thy lovingkindness: according unto the multitude of thy tender mercies blot out my transgressions. Wash me thoroughly from mine iniquity, and cleanse me from my sin. For I acknowledge my transgressions: and my sin is ever before me. Against thee, thee only, have I sinned, and done this evil in thy sight: that thou mightest be justified when thou speakest, and be clear when thou judgest. Behold, I was shapen in iniquity; and in sin did my mother conceive me"* (Psalm 51:1, 2). This was the glorious work of the Holy Spirit. Each person's path to God is different, yet the life of repentance and devotion to Christ always begin, following a visit from the Holy Spirit. The Spirit enlightens the soul, so it is able to see how crooked, guilty, and perverted it truly is. The human soul must be brought low before it can be lifted by the Gospel. By its understanding of human sin, the soul is miraculously led to the cross, and at the cross, the one being saved is able to acknowledge their guilt before their Creator and understand why the cross was needed and why Jesus had to sacrifice His life upon it. The cross confronts the sinner of their need for forgiveness and cleansing, while the blood of Christ proclaims the satisfied wrath of God upon His Son and the vile nature of human sin. Essentially, the cross conveys the story of human guilt and God's love for humanity despite us being completely undeserving... that's why it's such a good news.

The Gospel summarizes God's story to save His fallen creation from eternal destruction. It's a story that mysteriously began before the foundation of the earth and originated in heaven where sin was first conceived by Lucifer (Isaiah 14:12), one of God's guardian cherubs (Ezekiel 28:14). After the creation of Adam and Eve, Satan (Lucifer) was cast out of heaven and was given free reign upon the earth under the sovereignty of God. Thus, he arrived in the Garden of Eden to tempt, corrupt, and destroy God's perfect human race. Humanity was forever changed as the infection of original sin was, has, and still is being passed from person to person since that time. Throughout the years, God has worked to restrain human sin by destroying the world through a great flood, by creating new languages, by having abhorrent people groups and tribes killed, and most importantly, by establishing the people of Israel and giving them His law. It was the law that taught the Israelites—and the world for that matter—God's holiness, righteousness, and divine standards. These standards would separate them from the rest of the people groups on earth, allowing them to be His light in a fallen world. Ultimately, the law was added because of human sin until Jesus came into the world (Galatians 3:19) and has served as our guardian until His arrival so we could be justified by faith (Galatians 3:24) through His grace. Let us rejoice that justification has come through faith in Christ who has completely fulfilled the law (Matthew 5:17) for those who have come to trust in Him, His finished work, and His resurrection.

In summary, only a broken spirit can embrace the cross, a spirit like that of King David when the guilt of sin became so overwhelming and detestable that he cried out to God in confession and repentance. "Easy believism" in Jesus misleads the human soul into a dangerous life of false belief that will end in eternal hell. Becoming a soldier of the cross means a guaranteed life of mental and spiritual conflict, even death. Belief in the true Gospel will equip and then enlist you into Christ's army where you will fight against the great dragon under the leadership and guidance of Jesus Himself. Your life will be a pursuit of truth, a life of integrity, and self-denial.

Printed in the United States
By Bookmasters